Spirit Quest

The Hero's Journey

Best Wishes
Thistlewood

CORIN THISTLEWOOD

WITH ILLUSTRATIONS BY JEREMY HUGHES & STEPHANIE MINNS

Also by Corin Thistlewood
Chants of Power - Songs of Spirit
Introduction to Celtic Shamanism
Spirit Quest - The Hero's Journey
The Touchwood Chronicles trilogy
The Sun & the Moon
The Velum Scroll
Blue Moon Rising
Copyright © 2024 Corin Thistlewood

This is a work of fiction. Names, characters, places, and incidents either are the product of the author's imagination or are used fictitiously. Any resemblance to actual persons, living or dead, events, or locals is entirely coincidental.

Cover Design by Getcovers.com

All rights reserved. No part of this book may be reproduced or used in any manner without permission of the copyright owner except for use of quotations in a book review.

ISBN: 978-1-7394223-2-5 (paperback)
ISBN: 978-1-7394223-3-2 (eBook)

Dedication

To the growing number of Men's support groups that play a crucial role in addressing the lack of initiation for young men in modern society.

ILLUSTRATIONS

Chapter	Illustration	Artist
Cover	The Green Man	Steph Minns
1 Ivy	The Barrow	Steph Minns
1 Ivy	The Shaman on the Slab	Jeremy Hughes
2 Bramble	Salmon of Wisdom	Steph Minns
3 Apple	The old Shaman	Steph Minns
6 Oak	The green man	Steph Minns
6 Oak	Herculean Ogma	Jeremy Hughes
7 Hawthorn	Priestess of the Moon	Steph Minns
8 Willow	The Triple Goddess	Steph Minns
11 Rowan	Stay Awhile	Jeremy Hughes
13 Yew	Faces in the Trees	Steph Minns
13 Yew	Yew Mother	Steph Minns
16 Gorse	Wood Nymphs	Jeremy Hughes
16 Gorse	Corn & Grain - Dance	Jeremy Hughes
16 Gorse	Barrow Guardian Plays	Jeremy Hughes
17 Pine	Crown of Horns	Jeremy Hughes
18 Elder	Blessed Be Thy Feet	Jeremy Hughes
19 Blackthorn	The Winter Queen	Steph Minns
20 Reed	Moon Goddess	Steph Minns

Acknowledgements

Thanks to all the literally hundreds of people in Ireland, the UK and Australia whom I had the privilege to channel Ogham divination readings for and whose feedback validated the potency of the Ogham divination system I use.

Naomi Thistlewood: who had the patience to input to PC the original story from my scribbled handwritten notes.

Stephen Hobbs: a fellow druid whose down-to-earth knowledge of herb and tree lore has been invaluable to me. He also encouraged me to collect and carve wood from all twenty Ogham trees culminating in a unique and powerful divination set. With our combined knowledge we spent hours bouncing ideas off each other about Tree Lore, the Ogham and storytelling which ultimately resulted in the concept for this book.

Kaledon Naddair: who has contributed significantly to our understanding of Celtic heritage. He is the author of several books exploring Celtic folk and faerie tales whose work delves into the hidden meanings behind these. I have been particularly inspired by his work on the tree Ogham.

Finally, not least Jeremy Hughes & Stephanie Minns: who's wonderful artwork featured in this work, have added to its depth and brought the story alive as only a competent artist can.

Preface

The initial concept for this book came to me years ago when I was developing my interest in the Ogham and realised there was a whole host of associations attached to each sigil. Not only the designated native tree but all the tree lore associated with each one. But I was to learn that there was more. A lot more.

As an aside, if you are unsure as to just what the Ogham is, I have briefly outlined this in the appendix at the back of this book, together with a brief explanation of several other themes incorporated within this work.

However it was when I discovered the Wheel of Life, which is a Druid symbol representing the Celtic Medicine Wheel, that I found that each of the twenty trees had a position or 'station' about the wheel, it was only then that the full scope of the Ogham dawned on me. Each Ogham sigil had many associations. Even though the Ogham signs are named after twenty native trees which are the 'totem trees' for each sign. Linked to each Ogham there are also totem animals, birds, herbs, gods & goddesses, numbers, colours, mythic animals and a whole array of other associations intricately linked to the Celtic medicine wheel and important aspects of Celtic culture.

The ancient Druids had a taboo against the use of writing, so it follows the Ogham was never used as a written language as theirs was an oral tradition, passed on by word of mouth from druid to apprentice. They committed to memory immense amounts of poetry, this together with the Ogham was used by scholars as a mnemonic device for remembering their vast Lore. It was considered improper to commit their knowledge to writing, in case it should be vulgarised or corrupted and the memory of scholars become dimmed.

The poems and stories were recited publicly but without the 'knowledge of the trees' secreted within the Ogham, nothing could be gained by the uninitiated. The Ogham became the 'secret cypher' or 'keys' to their Lore and vast druid knowledge. So the Celtic Druids kept knowledge of the Ogham totally secret until their decline with the coming of the Roman invasion.

However the Romans never truly invaded Ireland so knowledge of the Ogham was never totally lost to druids and scholars. In fact, the Bardic Schools of Ireland continued till the middle of the 17th century providing what amounted to a university education in the arts.

So after discovering all this, the idea formed that the concept for this book was to follow the druid tradition and tell a good story, but woven within it are knowledge of the Ogham, the Celtic medicine wheel, together with many other aspects of Druidic and Wicca wisdom.

Myths and Lore surrounding the stag and the Stag King abound across the world and the millennia. From Meandash, the mythic Saami Reindeer, all the way back to the earliest history from Sumerian of Dara-Mah 'The Great Stag'. Today in common Wiccan duellist belief, The Horned God represents the male part, he is the consort of the female Triple goddess, and he is associated with nature, wilderness, sexuality, hunting, and the life cycle.

In Wicca too the narrative of the Wheel of the Year traditionally centres on the sacred marriage of the God and the Goddess. In this sacred mystery cycle, the God is perpetually reborn from the Goddess at Yule, the newborn sun at the winter solstice. As the young sun grows in power, it reaches its peak at the summer solstice. Then once again wanes in power till he passes into the underworld at Samhain. Hidden in the underworld he impregnates the Goddess. Until by some mystery, the new sun is once again born from Her mother/crone aspect at Yule.

So my story is set in the form of a hero quest or vision quest for a young man who sets out on this sacred journey only to discover the many aspects of himself and his spirituality. It is a rite of passage for a young man, who finds what it is to be a true man and learns to balance his male and female aspects becoming the mystical warrior. And through this the man becomes the Lord of all nature manifesting the power of the horned God through him. Only then can he become a worthy consort to a Goddess.

Corin Thistlewood

CHAPTER 1

Ivy

In the lands of the far north, the twilight of approaching dawn spreads a gloomy, unreal light over the landscape before us. A tall pointed finger of greyish-blue stone pointed skyward, standing among a forest of cedars, pines, birches, and oaks. Covered in green, yellow, blue, and brown lichens, the stone lifted from the forest floor and looked to be part of it, but was in fact much older. It was part of something mysterious and secret, almost forgotten.

Stags gathered here in springtime and scraped the velvet of their antlers against that stone. They would graze here—wild goats and sheep, too—causing the grass in the clearing to be cropped short like a lawn. But that was in the springtime.

Now snow lay thick on the ground. An icy wind blew savagely, causing deep drifts against anything that lay still. The forest's trees were heavily laden with snow. Their branches hanging low, almost breaking with the strain. The Winter Queen had passed her black rod over this land long ago, and she now reigned supreme. All life seemed to have stopped; it lay dormant.

An ancient long barrow lay concealed under the snow. Its black entrance was wide open, gaping like the mouth of a corpse. Before it lay a low, stone slab that could have been an altar; its sides were heavily carved with swirls and spirals. In the centre, a curious triple-spiral design demands our gaze.

Suddenly, out of the darkness, we hear excited shouts and the mournful sound of a bullhorn. Beyond the tree line, at the edge of the clearing, we can see glowing torches coming through the trees. A flurry of cloaks and long robes burst into the clearing. Out of their midst, half-leaping, half-running, comes a man, lightly clad in furs. In a frenzy, he tries to scramble up trees, rolls in the snow, and then leaps onto the carved slab. Crouching like an animal, his glazed, mad eyes stared this way and that.

"Quickly hold him on the stone... The little death will come over him soon," someone shouts with authority.

The group of men and women quickly catch up with the shaman on the slab; the many coloured robes circle to contain him. He surveys them with mad eyes, which, as we speak, glaze over, staring past them at something in the middle distance. His face contorted, barely able to form the words.

"... It comes..." With this utterance, he falls onto the stone, laying still, as if struck dead by an arrow through the heart.

The onlookers rush over to the stone. "He is ready," one proclaims.

"The oracle will speak soon."

"Emrys... Emrys, what do you see?"

Silence.

"Emrys... we must know if this winter will ever end."

The body on the slab shudders violently and then thrashes this way and that.

"Quick.... hold him still."

The shaman stops thrashing; his mouth is now forming words but with no sound. His whole body gives a sudden, horrifying jolt as if struck by something. Then he speaks in a loud, sing-song voice:

"... Tree snake spirals around the dead and dying... displays vibrant life

Spirit Quest: The Heros Journey

midst the deepest winter."

"The Oracle speaks," whispers the voice of authority.

"What is he saying?" A young man asks.

"Shh..." scolds the older man.

The shaman on the slab has tightly closed eyes but shakily points at the sky with a gnarled finger, uttering, "... Its berries provide nourishment for starving birds."

"Is he talking of the vision potion he has taken?"

"Maybe... quiet; he speaks again."

"... I see a child; he rides a boat in the sea of reeds..."

"This is no vision of the future; we found a boy child in the Reed bed last moon... We all know it."

"Quiet Gelban; we need to hear."

"... Ivy clings to its host... like a child to its mother... Guard him well, for the sun shines from his brow." The shaman's eyes suddenly open, staring seemingly at nothing, then whispers, ".... Deep in the earth the dragon stirs... on Brides morn' the serpent shall come from the hole." With this last utterance, the shaman falls silent, wasted by his efforts.

"The stone has spoken; praise be!"

"Tis true, the sun will at last return; praise be to the old Gods; praise be to the Goddess." Hurriedly, they cover the shaman with furs, carry him back to the village to sleep it off, and warm themselves by the fire. Each was deep in thought about what had been spoken.

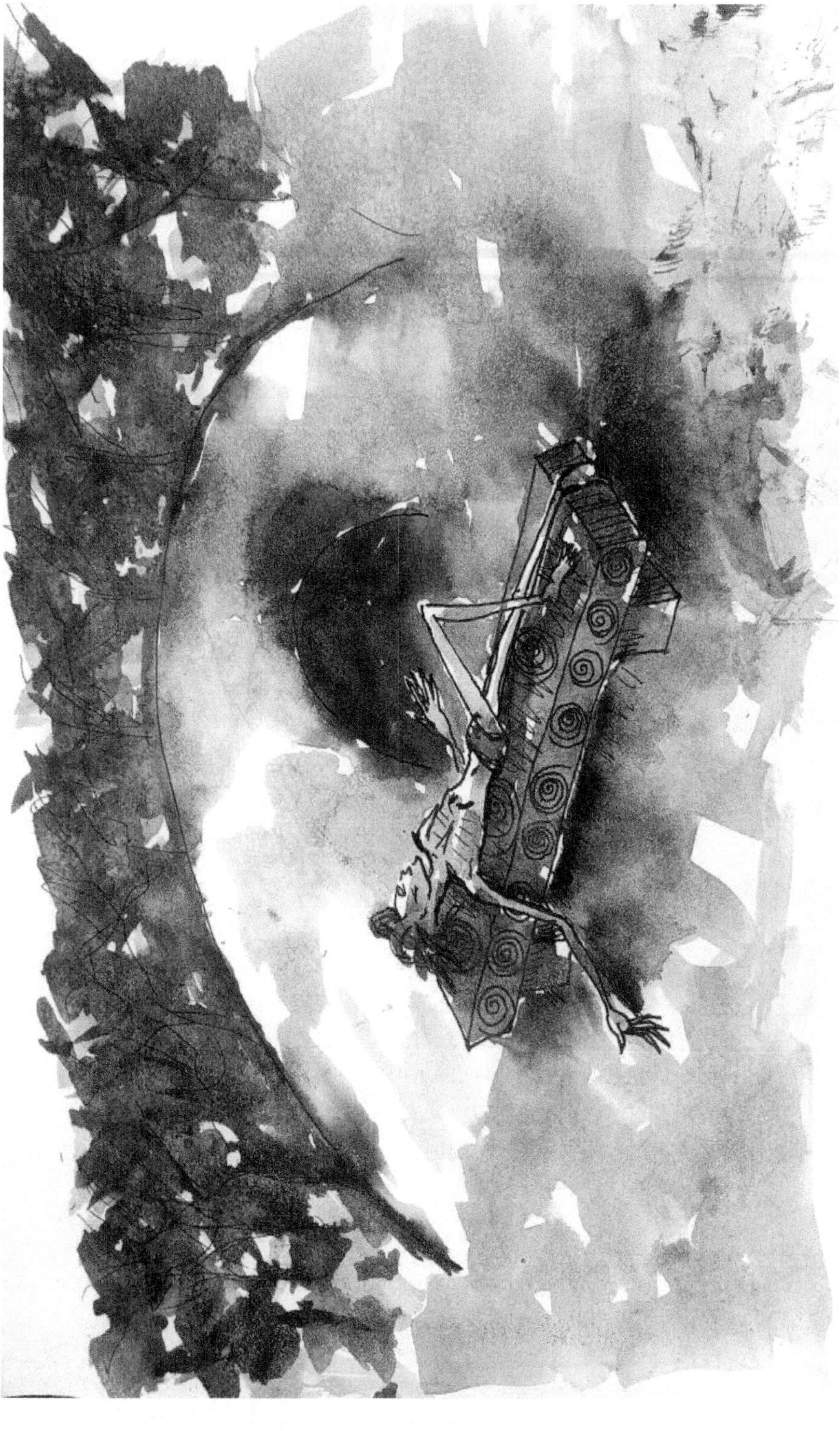

CHAPTER 2

Bramble

It was the eve of the festival of Brigid. The early-morning ceremonies had gone well, but now the evening celebrations would continue well into the night. Fresh country ale and wine flowed freely, as there was little in the way of food after the ravages of winter.

Since the winter solstice, the sun has been steadily gaining strength, and soon the first signs of new growth will be anticipated.

Oisin, a tall and cheerful boy, brought another jug of ale to the feasting table. It was the custom of the older children to help out on such occasions. Oisin set the jug down before two large men, who bore the alms of the warrior class.

"Ahh! More ale praise thee... 'tis young Oisin, or should I say, 'The boy from the Reeds'. I see the old Shaman has taken a shine to you, my lad."

"Leave the boy alone... He's brought more joy and happiness to that old man than I ever thought possible," said the older warrior.

"Here, boy, let's see you down some of this blackberry wine; that'll make a man of you," said one warrior.

"Or an ass, if he has too much". Said the other warrior, laughing loudly.

Oisin was of an age where they were keen to demonstrate that they were grown up and no longer a child. So without thinking, he quickly snatched the offered wine skin and gulped down the strong country wine as if it were water. But never having drunk alcohol before, he didn't realize its potency. The two warriors laughed heartily at the amusing spectacle, then turned back to the feast, leaving Oisin feeling slightly foolish.

By this time, it was late into the night - almost dawn. Oisin had had enough of the festivities and decided to go for a walk to greet the dawn on his own. After walking for a while, the eastern sky gradually grew lighter. Oisin, deep in thought, started thinking about the things he wanted to do this coming summer.

... It came from the woods in the north, a whispering piping that set the hairs at the nape of his neck tingling. At first, Oisin thought it was some kind of bird song but soon realized that no bird could make such an air. As he listened, its melody dipped and shifted, sometimes low, and breathy, now high, and skirling. It was always low and quiet, just on the edge of hearing, as it would scamper up and down the music scale, shimmering and lilting, unlike any bird.

But now his head had started to spin; the strong wine was taking effect. His vision started to blur, and he began to stagger, feeling slightly sick. He had a rising feeling, and things didn't feel quite right; his body didn't seem to belong to him anymore. Everything about him began to swirl around and around as he staggered down the path.

Suddenly, an adder darts out from a hole under a large rock, straight across his path. Startled and suddenly brought to his senses, he leaps backwards, straight into a patch of brambles. On his back, he lies there among the blackberry vines, held fast by the vicious barbs; feeling pricks of pain all over his body. Suddenly, cold-sober, staring up at the sky, he could see the full moon shining brightly above him.

'How beautiful she looks' Oisin thought to himself, forgetting for a moment where he was. Had there been any actual sound? Listening hard, he strained to hear it again, but there was nothing but the low murmuring of the wind...

The suggestion of music must have been from within. But as soon as he relaxed again, he felt assured that it was not. Most certainly from without, but not by any sense of hearing. A new feeling passed over him, revelry, dance, and splendour poured into him—no sound. Yet in such a fashion that it could only be remembered or thought of except as music. It was like having a new sense; it was like being present when the morning stars sang together. It was as if the earth at that moment had been re-created—and perhaps, in a sense, it had.

At the same moment, he was conscious of a sense of triumph. But it was not him who was triumphant; the whole darkness around him rang with victory. But sweeter than all the sensations was the suggestion that he had been brought there not to do anything but only as a spectator or a witness.

He looked up at the moon again, cold and clear in the frosty air; a multicoloured halo surrounded it. But as he watched, a dark silhouette sailed across the face of the moon. It looked like a woman astride a long black staff, but then it was gone. Searching around the sky to find her again, he was just in time to see her circle around and land just before him, beside a small pool of water.

Oisin was fascinated; clearly, she hadn't seen him in the brambles. The old woman dismounts her long black staff and hides it under a nearby Holly bush. Satisfied, she then walks over to the water's edge. Pausing for a while to regard the reflection of the moon in the water, she then plunges deep into the pool. Before his bemused eyes, the old hag of winter transforms into a long-necked swan.

The swan ruffles her snowy white feathers, then glides gracefully across the pool. Oisin could not believe what his eyes told him; he thought he must be dreaming. 'Yes, that was it,' he thought, 'the strong wine had made him fall asleep... in a patch of brambles! How strange".

Slowly and painfully, he unravels himself from the barbarous brambles and goes over to the pool's edge to drink and wash his face. As he approaches, the swan swims over to the security of the rushes on the other side of the pool.

'T'is a strange thing to happen on a beautiful morning,' he thinks to himself. 'T'is strange too that in all my childhood exploring, I hadn't seen or heard of such a pool, surrounded by Hazel trees as it is. T'is magical, so it is.'

The brambles had made some nasty scratches on his body, so he decided to undress and bathe them in the pool. The water is icy but refreshing for his tender wounds. Carefully, he washes the blood from his skin.

Eventually, feeling cleansed, he climbs out of the pool, dresses, and decides to return to his village and a warm bed. With one last look back at the mysterious pool, he just catches sight of a rainbow-coloured salmon leaping into the air. With the early morning sunlight glistening on its wet skin. It seems to hang there for a moment before plunging back into the shimmering water. Oisin smiles and continues home, marvelling at the wonder and beauty of nature.

When the boy had gone and all was quiet, the white swan swam out of the rushes towards the edge of the pool. As she emerges from the water, the swan shimmers and shifts into the shape of the beautiful, naked swan maiden. The young bride of spring emerges at the dawn of the year to reawaken the seeds of nature.

Spirit Quest: The Heros Journey 15

CHAPTER 3

Apple

Under the watchful eye and guidance of his mentor and foster father, the old Shaman, Oisin is growing into a fine young boy, showing promise in all he does. Oisin is apprenticed to the Shaman and is learning the old ways, the world of the unseen.

The tribal chief too has taken a shine to him and is training him in alms and other warrior craft which to the shaman's ire Oisin seems more interested in. Young Oisin puts his heart into and excels at wrestling, swordplay, and other sports such as hurling.

It was the eve of the winter festival of remembrance, the eve of Samhain when all would remember the tribal ancestors. All those souls that had gone before, that had pair bonded and had made their hearth fires. Those that had brought new children into the tribe to make it strong and allow it to grow.

Those Great tribal chiefs and Hero warriors who protected the tribe in times of crisis would be remembered also. It was for these that food would be laid out before the ancient barrows, whose Great stones would be removed; so that the dead knew they would be welcome, this one night about the camp fires.

Oisin, like so many of the young people, cared nothing for all of this. All that concerned him was that it was another opportunity for the boys to show off in front of the girls, at a social gathering. He was not unaware of the attentions of many of the younger girls in his tribe, some much younger than he. They had seen how good he was at the games and were attracted to the older boy.

One young girl in particular catches his eye, though much younger than he, barely eleven summers. She has long black plaited hair and green eyes with high cheekbones. Beneath her thin linen shift the promise of her young womanhood clearly budding, as she holds her shoulders back every time Oisin looks over. He notices that she looks at him in a very 'interesting', way which causes strange stirrings in his manhood. He is determined to impress her, this night.

At the 'dooking' for Apples contest he feels confident he can win her an Apple. So, when it is his turn he kneels before the Great Cauldron, his hands tied behind his back. In anticipation, he looks down into the water glistening and swirling in the torchlight.

Many juicy apples of green and red bobbing like corks on a stormy sea. Apple is the promise of your heart's desire, such tempting fruit, so many to choose.

Oisin looks up again and catches the girl looking at him again with great interest, her green eyes glowing in the torchlight, coyly she looks away. Oisin is determined, his head goes down trying first one apple then another, then another, all evades his searching mouth.

He tries again, and again but without success. In anger he dives at an apple, almost falling in the cauldron his head goes completely below the water. He comes up for air gasping and spluttering, with no apple; to the wild laughter from everyone else.

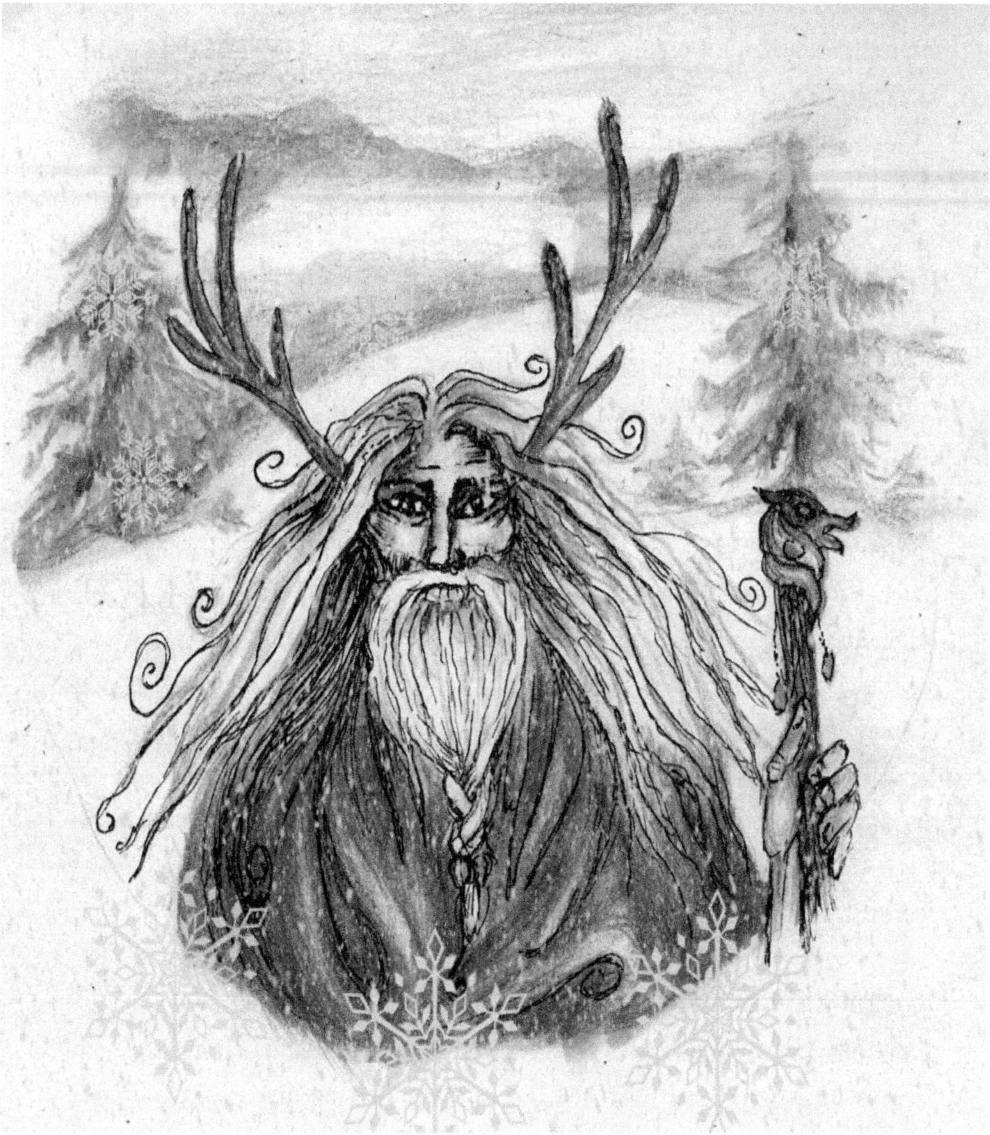

Deeply embarrassed Oisin looks about him wildly and then observes one who is not laughing. A face beyond the fire light deep in the shadows. The old, wrinkled face of Emrys the Shaman his teacher. Oisin stares for a moment and then lowers his head racing from the room to peals of laughter from the crowd.

Outside the boy runs to his hut and his sleeping furs. In a fit of anguish, he falls into a deep troubled sleep.

... In his dreams the face of the Shaman appears again, red and flickering in the fire light, sometimes seeming to fade altogether. The Shaman speaks, but the mouth does not move

... "Fire naturally rises, water naturally settles... Apple is the promise of your heart's desire, such tempting fruit. So many to choose from... young woman at first menses... find herself experimenting with her new 'woman's' body... in a childish way...Not realizing its power... not realizing she is playing with fire.... makes a play to older boys... may take this play/tease other than intended... When dooking for apples in life's Cauldron... symbolic of the good things life has to offer... make our choice and concentrate on this... Perseverance in a course of action leads to Our goal... jump... jump... jump spreads our energies too thinly... leads only to dissatisfaction... Choose one and enjoy it to the full... This is a lesson to learn from nature... 'Perseverance and continuity is change'... this is the secret of the eternity of the Universe...

Oisin who has been tossing and turning in his furs suddenly wakes up, perspiration dripping from his brow, the bright sunlight shining through the smoke hole. A new day has begun. Troubled by his dream, he goes quietly to his breakfast.

.

CHAPTER 4

Hazel

Oisin awoke with a start; he blinked sleepily as the bright sunshine poured in from the door flap. The grizzled form of the old shaman could be seen silhouetted as he called, "Come my boy what hour do you call this? You sleepy head, the Sun has risen over the mountains already and we have work to do".

"W.....what?' Oisin managed sleepily.

"You look like a dormouse waking from a winter's sleep," chided the shaman. "What ails 'ye this morning?" He almost cantered over to the boys' sleeping furs and pulled them back. "There you are, rise and shine."

Oisin groaned at the rude awakening, as the old man went outside for a moment, returning with two steaming bowls of herbal tea. Sitting down next to the bed, he offered one to Oisin, who sleepily accepted.

"Our services are needed," the medicine man continued more kindly. "One of the villages over the ridge-way there has gone dry, or their well has, they need us to dowse for a new well site for them." His eyes looked to the sky, shaking his head, "The Oracle told them about this three summers ago, but would they listen...? Anyway, we need to be off, it's half a day's walk to get there: with my old legs." With that, he stood up and bounded out of the doorway like a spring lamb.

"Come on" he shouted from outside the doorway.

Oisin staggered out of his hut and trotted after the wise man, his feet tripping and stumbling.

They walked in silence for some way. Oisin had woken up now and was striding beside the old Druid; unexpectedly he broke the silence. "You see, first we need to cut a fresh hazel twig - for the finding of the water. Well... I find the water, the twig is just to impress the villages. Ye see if I was to just tell them to dig where I felt was the right place...? Well somehow, they need all the hocus pocus - that way they feel the gods are with them... know what I mean". With this comment, he had placed his right index finger along the ridge of his nose and tapped it.

Oisin had come to learn that this was a secret signal to indicate the start of something hidden that was passed between two Druids. He knew that there was some sort of secret language that they used, but he was not ready to learn it just yet. But with this gesture, he knew that he was being taught some of the 'tricks of the trade.'

"That's not to say," the old man continued, "that novice diviners don't need the twigs at first, 'cos they do. But you sort of, outgrow them... sort of. Well, you'll see when you do it for yourself."

"What me?"

"Yes, you. But don't fret I'll be able to come along later to do all the trickery with the twig and confirm it"

They had been walking steadily for some time, up a gradual incline. Just as they neared the top, Oisin could see a stranger approaching them along the road.

"Oh! Columb, 'tis nice to see you this beautiful morning," shouted the Druid.

"Ah!" Exclaimed the chieftain, "That's strange, I was just coming to see you... Our villagers are in a bit of a state 'Cos our... "

"Main well has dried up?"

"Y... Yes... and the alternative supply is over two miles away and the woman... Say how'd you...? Well, I suppose you are the Shaman."

All the while, the old man had been looking at Columb with a bemused look on his face. As he saw the penny drop in the chieftain, he burst out laughing, as did Columb. And Oisin, after a few seconds of bemused silence, joined them. The old Druid never ceased to amaze him. Just when he had started to think the old man was getting past it or senile... Like earlier this week, when he had taken Oisin to a good place to cut hazel twigs.

... They had been walking through a wood when the Shaman suddenly stopped, "Do you see it?"

"See what...? Oh, I see a clearing in the trees"

"No. Look but don't look, use your blind eye, the one inside your head... like I showed you before"

Oisin had tried, as the Shaman had shown him, breathing deeply and closing his eyes. Ever so gradually, the clearing appeared in his mind.

"That's it. Now walk to those willow trees over there and look at the clearing through them. They're what we call a 'gateway'."

Oisin had done as he was instructed. Yes... gradually he could see a wondrous sight shimmering before him, a crystal-clear pool of water surrounded by nine hazel trees. As he stood transfixed, a Salmon leapt out of the water, its scales glistening in the ethereal light, creating rainbows across its body.

"I have seen this place before," Oisin exclaimed excitedly. "... there was a... "

"Yes, yes," interrupted the shaman. "I know well of your vision, it is a place I go to often; a sacred place of inspiration. You too will come here again when the need arises. But for the moment we come here for another reason; to cut you a staff. All travellers on the path we tread, need their staff. So listen closely and listen well, for our time here is limited.

"Hazel is the venerated tree of the Sidhe; 'The Gentry'. We come to them for help sometimes. And... if it suits them they may give it; but always at a price. This place where we are now is called the Otherworld. If we cut a living staff here and bring it back to our world, we can then use it to 'connect' to this place. For we do not want to linger here; for here there are hidden dangers."

Oisin was listening closely but felt his throat tighten at the shaman's words. But the wise man continued.

"This sacred, magical spring is surrounded by nine hazel trees. In the pool, there are five salmon. They are the 'salmon of wisdom' who eat of the nuts that fall into its waters. These nuts are said to contain the feats of the ancient Sages - Knowledge of all the arts and sciences. They are the embodiment of concentrated wisdom and poetic inspiration.

"We humans are not permitted to eat of the fruit of that particular tree, but wisdom can come to us through the Salmon. Now, our living staff may be likened to a magical wand, for by some mystery, it can act as a conduit for the serpent fire; the telluric energies of the earth. This too may bring us wisdom, for it cuts through all the crap in the mundane world, all the muddles that dark-minded people create. Almost magically gets to the gist of the subject, focusing the problem; 'in a nutshell' so to speak. Thus, allowing the concentrated wisdom of the ages to flow through it and thus to you."

The old shaman stopped for a moment, placing his hand on the base of the boy's neck. Oisin could feel a revitalising warmth and energy flow through him.

"Now," the shaman continued, "I have already shown you how to 'feel' the aura, the life force about people. We can also do it with trees. Hold up your hands and feel the Aura of that Hazel tree there. Now, count the bands as you walk in. At five introduce yourself to the tree; make friends with your brother the tree. At three state your intent and ask permission to cut a wand, if you feel you are accepted and the tree is happy with this arrangement, continue till you touch the bark.

"Now 'meld' with it like I taught you with the frog, remember? Feel the strength of it, feel the life force surging through it. Then, ask for it to indicate where we need to cut, to get our wand. It is here that a tiny fragment of the tree spirit will reside and become your ally. When you know where to cut, hold your hands on either side of the place and concentrate. Imagine the cut there, see the 'light' in the tree split apart between your hands. Then carefully and quickly cut it with your knife. Remembering, as I showed you before to heal the stump; apologizing to the tree for any distress we may have caused. We will work and consecrate the staff when we get home. Have you got all that? Work away"

... Standing there on the road, Oisin mused to himself that he had never seen the shaman quite so energized and clear-thinking as he had been in that 'Otherworld.

Suddenly coming to his senses, he looked up just in time to see the two men some-way ahead walking around a bend and disappearing from view. Quickly, he trotted off after them; he didn't want to risk another scolding.

CHAPTER 5

Holly

As time passed, the boy Oisin had grown into a tall youth. He was straight and tough, like a Holly-shafted spear. He seemed confident too in everything that he undertook, excelling at arms and swordplay. He had a strong spear arm; his aim was straight and true. He looked good, too, on the hurling field, displaying his strong arm and leg muscles and employing his keen eye, winning many games.

He was much admired by his tribe. All loved him for being a model warrior. Yes, he was loved, and not more so than by several young girls who eyed his firm young body on the playing field. One young girl in particular, Talisa had one day caught his eye. Now they could often be seen talking together or walking at the edge of the village; clearly, she liked him, too.

"She has the eye of one who would have him for a husband," declared Ulla, the tribal chief, as he stood arms folded warming his broad backside by the central fire. It was a chilly spring evening and the central fire was the traditional meeting place after the work of the day. People would gather eager for their evening meal. Ulla smiled indulgently as he watched young Oisin approaching, young Talisa giggling and chatting on his arm.

"Aye, I had noticed" replied the old Shaman gravely.

Ulla stopped grinning and turned to the old man, "You don't approve?"

"Aye. I do approve. 'Tis surely every young man's right..."

"But?" Ulla's piercing grey eyes regarded the old man questioningly.

"But 'tis not his destiny... he is bound for... for, 'other things,'" countered the old Shaman vaguely. Even he felt uncomfortable under the steely glare of the tribal chief's eyes.

"But surely there are no greater riches than the love of a good woman and... and a son on your knee," stated Ulla convincingly; he could be like a terrier worrying a bone if he got his teeth into an argument.

"That may be true... aye true," the old man was visibly cringing now. But gathered his courage, saying, "But... she's not the one"

"But surely that is for those two to decide," countered the chieftain.

The old Shaman had been dreading this moment for some time, for surely, he knew it would come. He knew, too, that he would need to be tactful with this proud chieftain. "He is one who is... 'fated'... err... the 'Weavers' would have it otherwise... I have seen it... They have given me... visions."

Ulla was quiet for a while, for he feared such things that the shaman talked about. But eventually replied, "such as he will need strong guidance"

"We have not spoken of this before but... but 'tis time you knew, for he is.... 'The chosen one.'"

"You mean...?"

"Yes, the boy from the reeds is to be the sacrificial king." Now the shaman could relax; the worst was over. "I have seen his shining brow when we went to cut his staff."

Ulla looked grave. "He may turn against us when you tell him."

"When, I, tell him...?" The Shaman stood poker-faced but had a mischievous glint in his eye.

"Surely not I...?" Ulla stuttered and turned to the shaman with a worried look. But seeing the old man's twinkling eye, laughed with relief.

"He will learn for himself before long Ulla... 'Tis in the stars. But I need you to train him all the harder and be very firm with him. I too will play my part." With this the Shaman turned toward the great food cauldron bubbling over the fire, receiving a steaming bowl of broth gratefully. He spoke not another word for the rest of the night.

Ulla, too, received his portion of broth. But sat silently staring into it for a long time; before finally laying it down on the ground for the dogs.

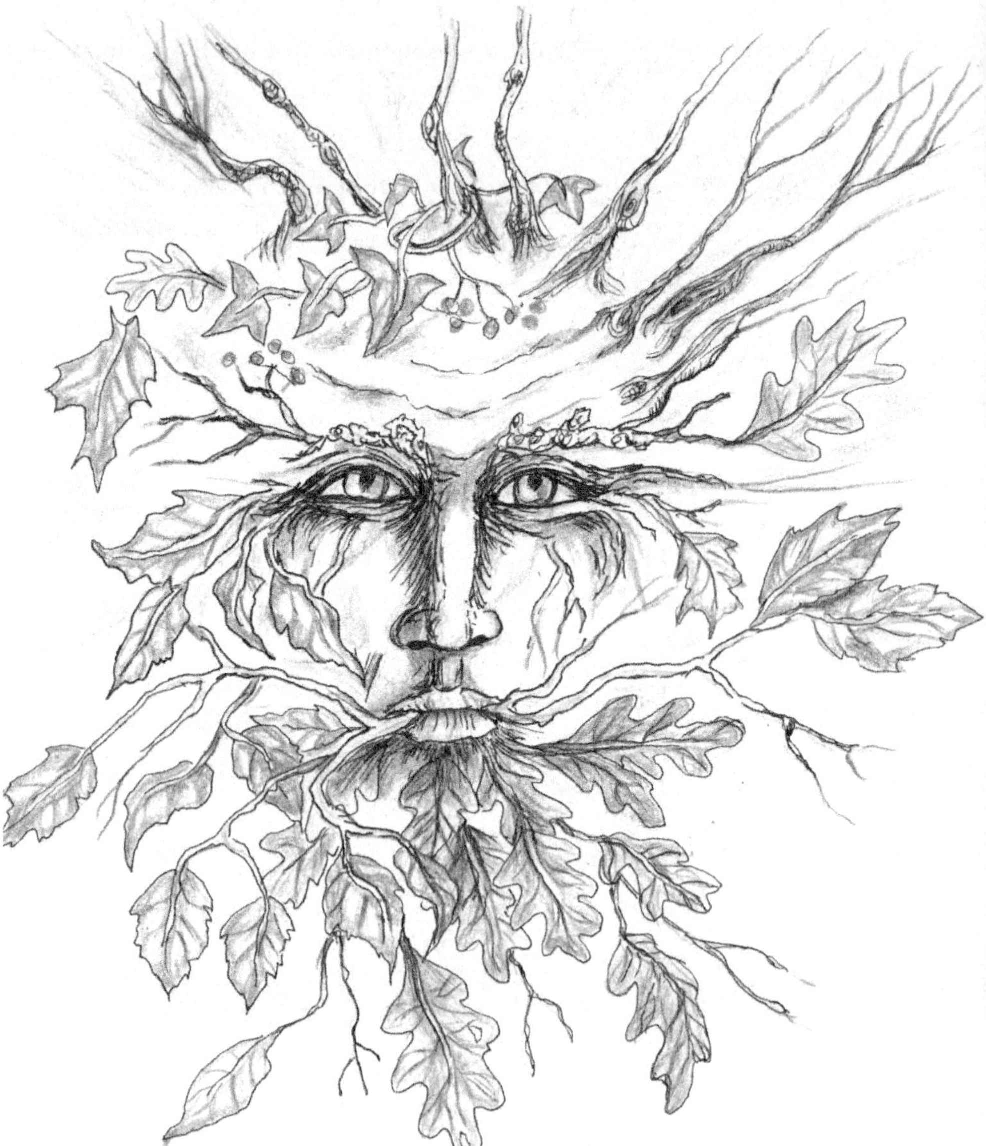

CHAPTER 6

Oak

The young man who some called 'Oisin' stood before the Great Forest that stretched before him. He had known many who ventured into its Darkness; few had returned. He stood with the tribal Elder on one side and the ancient shaman on his other. Both wore long white beards - but he knew that beneath this facial hair lay the tribal scars of their manhood.

For many years he had been trained well on the significance of this ritual he was about to undergo. Yet it seemed like only yesterday, he had been the 'chosen one', the 'Sun king', cherished and honoured among his people. He was the 'golden boy'. He remembered how he always seemed to excel at all the games of skill and laughed from victory to victory. He was the living triumph of youth and strength, and his people loved him for it.

But today. Today, he was hardly able to contain his fear as the two elder men drew their long black horns and sounded them in unison. Three times the call went out, three times the 'call of the wild'. Then the whole forest seemed to fall silent in anticipation.

At first, he thought it was some kind of bird song, but then he recognized it for the low whispering music he had heard before. Reedy piping, so low that if you were not listening intently, you could miss it altogether. The music was full of deep leafy woods full of bracken, a thick forest floor of rich humus, with an aroma more intoxicating than freshly ground coffee.

The music spoke of a faint hint of deer musk on the wind. Of nights when the thin clouds raced across the hare-faced Moon and of its bright silvery light pouring down illuminating old, gnarled tree boughs and the faces of your brothers and sisters stood in circle in a forest clearing. The music spoke of these things and much more.

Suddenly, there was a loud animalistic bellow as if from a wild Bull or a Stag. Before him, the trees started to quiver and shake and the thunderous sound of a huge club beating on the hollow trees echoed throughout the forest.

Oisin stared transfixed. It sent thrills of exquisite horror tingling along his spine. Surely his eyes were deceiving him as he beheld the apparition that had emerged from the forest. The Giant Stag stood there taller than a man. With antlers of seven tines majestically towering like twin trees above him.

Never had he seen such a beast. Yet, as he watched, it shimmered and changed. The terrified boy squinted, blinked and screwed up his eyes, looking sideways, trying to focus clearly on the beast. One minute it was the Giant Stag, then there was a man's body with the stag's head. Next, he could see the head change to a goat, then a man's head with a goat's legs. Constantly, it shifted and changed. Once he saw a wild boar, with a bristling back and large tusks.

But gradually the vision became more clearly defined. There, stood a tall Giant of a man, brandishing a huge Oak club. His body was lean and hard and was quite naked, except for some greenery wrapped about, which seemed to sprout from his very skin, as did the soft reddish hair, which grew thickly all over. His magnificent phallus hung heavily below a mass of dark curls. His powerful thighs rippled with strength as he walked towards them. He had strong Teutonic features with weathered skin, toned with

Spirit Quest: The Heros Journey

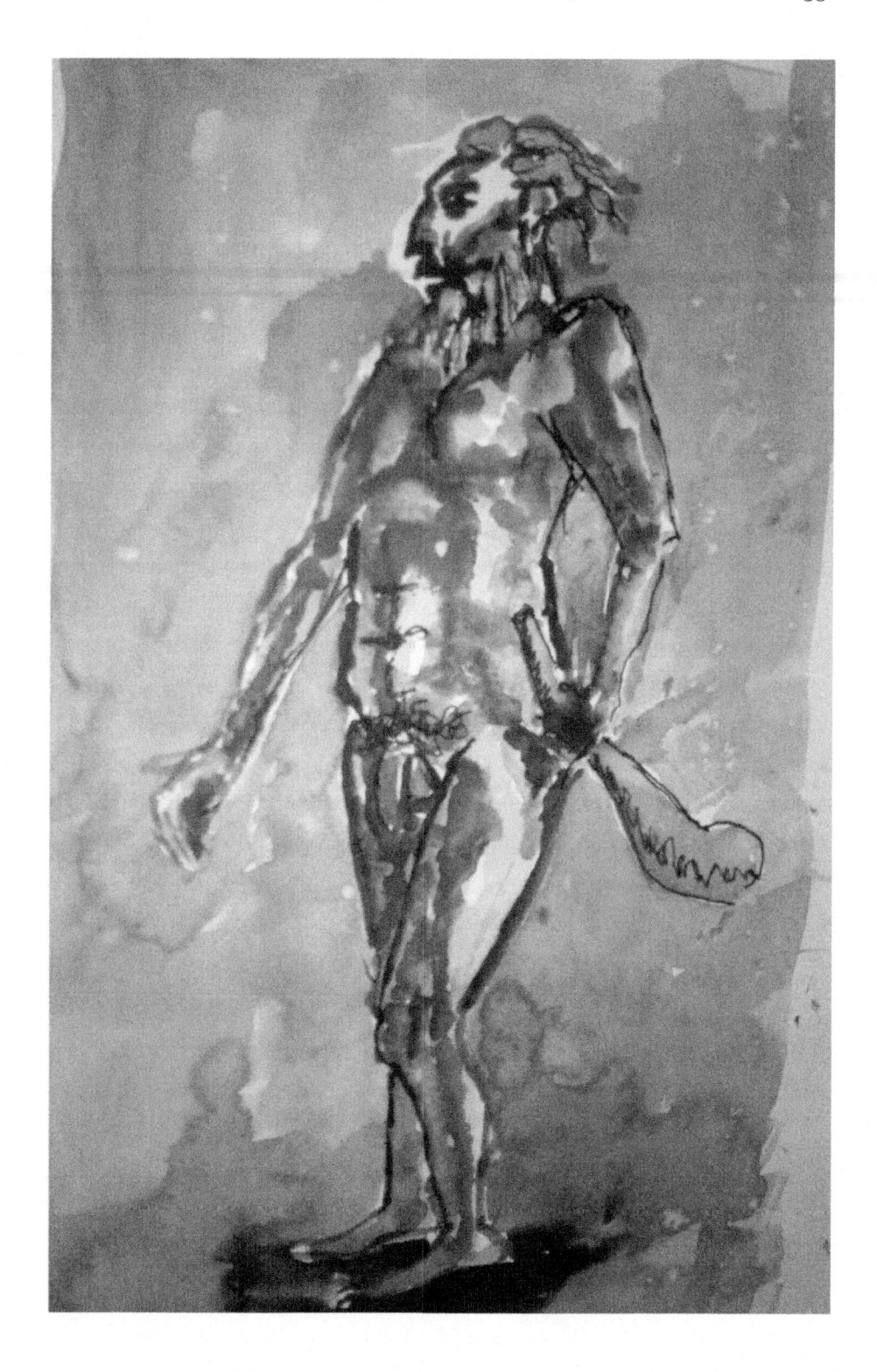

colours of the earth. A broad nose and brow, deep-set eyes and his large mouth with thick lips gave a wide smile that matched the humorous glint of his deep brown eyes.

Oisin knew at once that this was the Green Man of the forest, the ancient Herculean God whom some called Ogma, and many other names. All the while the two Elders had been muttering incantations, but as the God stopped before them, they ceased and stepped gingerly to one side.

Somehow, this magnificent being that stood before Oisin, who now looked him straight in the eyes, seemed to both terrify, yet fill him with a powerful calmness and strength. Unspoken messages passed between them for what seemed like an eternity. Somehow, he was able to communicate to the boy, what it was to be a man of courage, bravery, and strength. To have the ability to overcome and survive, coupled with strength of purpose.

Yes, these were all there, but so too was the wildness, the fecundity, the gentleness, the caring and protecting self - the nurturer and respecter of women; guardian of tribe and family.

All this passed between them. Slowly Ogma raised his mighty club with both hands, high above the boy's head, then lowered it gently, first on his left shoulder, then his right. Untold feelings passed through him. Somehow Oisin understood for a brief moment the essential essence of this God. His compassion, his patience for humankind, the children of the God and Goddess. How slowly we learn, how easily we forget...

Then the Green Man removed his club and the feelings passed. The two Elders now stepped forward and produced small sickle-shaped knives. The boy tensed, feeling bile rising from his gut - for he knew what was coming next.

Skilfully and quickly, the Shaman made three small cuts on Oisin's right thigh, the symbol of his totem animal. Then the tribal Elder made two more, one on each cheek, that was to make a statement to the world that he had been initiated into the male mysteries. Oisin was no longer a boy; he had now entered the world of men.

As the Elders dabbed white ash onto his wounds, Oisin watched the Herculean figure slowly walk back to the trees, tears slowly welling in his eyes. Just before the God merged with the forest, he turned to look back. Was that a wink? Oisin looked again, but no, 'twas only the stirring of the leaves on an old Oak tree.

Slowly, the three returned to the village. But all the way home, Oisin couldn't help but wonder, would he be worthy, would he remember all the Green Man had taught him...

CHAPTER 7

Hawthorn

They stood on a rise of small hills that looked down onto the ancient forest. It stretched uninterrupted as far as the eye could see in all directions. Huge, ancient, twisted Oak and Yew, tall Pine, Alder, and Ash; all the native trees were there.

The priestess of the moon and the young man called Oisin stood alone, save for the sacred thorn. Its coloured rags, feathers, beads, and shells fluttered gently in the breeze; a testimony to the sacredness of this place and his people's faith in the beneficial powers of the Faerie.

As he surveyed the ancient forest, Oisin reminisced...

Only a few short days before, the ancient shaman, his mentor and tutor had looked at him strangely for a long time. Initially, the look had been one of joy and pride, of a father for his son. But then a glint of salt water formed in his rheumy eyes as he somberly walked over to the boy. The shaman had simply asked him to follow; naturally, Oisin obeyed.

He had led him to a small round hut just outside the village. It had always been there, but Oisin knew that only woman-folk had been allowed to enter. Now he had been left to stand before the small round doorway. It was a simple hut. Just above the doorway was an ancient wooden carving of an old woman squatting as if giving birth. She was holding open her own Vulva. Oisin couldn't help but think how Vulva-like this narrow doorway was, as he crouched down on his hands and knees to enter.

It was dark inside the hut, but there was just enough light from a small fire to see. An old woman was sitting on the other side of the fire pit. She was incredibly old, older than anyone he had ever seen. Around her neck were many cords with a multitude of bones and teeth attached. But also, he noticed a small bone carving of the same Sheela-na-Gig figure he had seen above the doorway.

Silently, she gestured with her hand for him to sit on the door side of the fire pit. She sat in silence while observing him for what seemed like a very long time. Then, as if a decision had been made, she ladled some liquid from a pot simmering beside the fire, into a small bowl and laid it down on the stones, gesturing for him to take it. Passively, he obeyed and sipped. It was some 'remedy' made from woodland fungus, which he had not tasted before and was quite unpleasant. But not wanting to offend, he had slowly sipped it till it was gone. Only then did the old woman speak, but with a surprisingly young voice.

"There are some people who are genuinely willing to make real sacrifices for others. But often generosity is not selfless; sometimes generous acts are expected to bring a certain return. This is truly a time of increase for you, because in the past 'others' - your ancestors, were willing to make real selfless sacrifices for the common good. To give and not receive - to let go of something of themselves without expecting something to replace it.

"You have been chosen; your spiritual path is one of self-sacrifice. You are the Sun king. Not for you is a young wife with her hearth fire, or to bear children as your friends and Kin folk have done. No, it is your path to leave your family, your heart fire - your home - to venture on a Vision Quest. On that Quest you will experience many things; you will lose yourself and find the God within"

She had continued talking for a long time and as he stared into the fire, gradually everything else had faded and the only thing he was aware of was

39

the hypnotic words of the wise Woman. Much of it he could not comprehend. Some he had forgotten, but the words still lay within him, and as time passed, he understood more and more...

But now he stood here before the ancient forest, about to venture on that Great Quest, alone.

CHAPTER 8

Willow

The priestess of the moon walked back to the village. Oisin watched her as she slowly walked away. Her long, silvery robe hardly seemed to move as the young priestess glided silently along the path. It was She; who had led him to this place. She; who had cropped his long golden locks, which now lay at his feet. She; who had taken his fine kilt and vestment. Only the simple golden torc remained around his neck.

Nothing else had she allowed him, no weapons, no food. He stood there naked and vulnerable. Turning back to the vast ancient forest, he saw that it stretched in every direction; as far as the eye could see. What dangers lay hidden in its depths, he could not tell. Although he had heard many a tale about the strange happenings to people who entered that Great Forest. Although most were tales from long ago.

A sudden wind blew up, bringing with it cold rain. It blew hard on his skin, soaking him through and chilling him to the bone. He knew he could not return to the village. The forest, although uninviting, would afford some protection, at least from the elements.

And so, this was how the young man, Oisin, entered the next phase of life's journey. He had entered the forest with great foreboding; its dark depths looked uninviting, but he knew he had no other place to go. As he followed the deep pathway under the overhanging branches, the rain continued. It was a thin, cold, misty rain that penetrated to the bone. It threaded and beaded every branch, leaf, and twig. Dripped mournfully down tree trunks and created little rivulets down the banks at either side of the road. The banks were nearly as high as a walled house and were laced and knotted with enormous, twisted roots all overgrown with moss and little dripping tongues of fern.

Oisin kept looking up at the sky, in the hope of seeing a break in the clouds. But the great arching boughs of the trees met overhead and shut out the sky almost completely. In silence, he continued walking through the Great Forest for the remainder of the day.

Towards dusk, the rain eased off, but this only brought new menaces. While it rained, at least, the forest had been silent and almost devoid of life. But now there seemed to be great looming green shadows everywhere he looked. All about him, there was creaking and groaning. The crack of a broken twig, the creak of a tree, or a loose stone falling down the bank. In the glooming twilight, under the great trees, his eyes began playing tricks on him. As moving leaves waved and shifted in the uncertain light. One old stump in particular, a little way off, covered in ivy, looked exactly like a hooded figure in a green cloak, all hunched over like an old man. And no doubt about it, there were several pairs of bright little yellow eyes, blinking at him from holes in the bank. But these, he tried to assure himself, were rabbits or vixens or some such animal.

As darkness came, he set up camp beside a small stream. He had collected sparking stones along the way; having been taught well, how to survive in the natural world. Lighting a fire, he lay back exhausted against a massive willow tree. Although he hadn't eaten that day, the flames were comforting. Now his mind began to think about the day and the great journey ahead and how he had come to be here.

Watching the flames flicker and dance, he was reminded of the day he

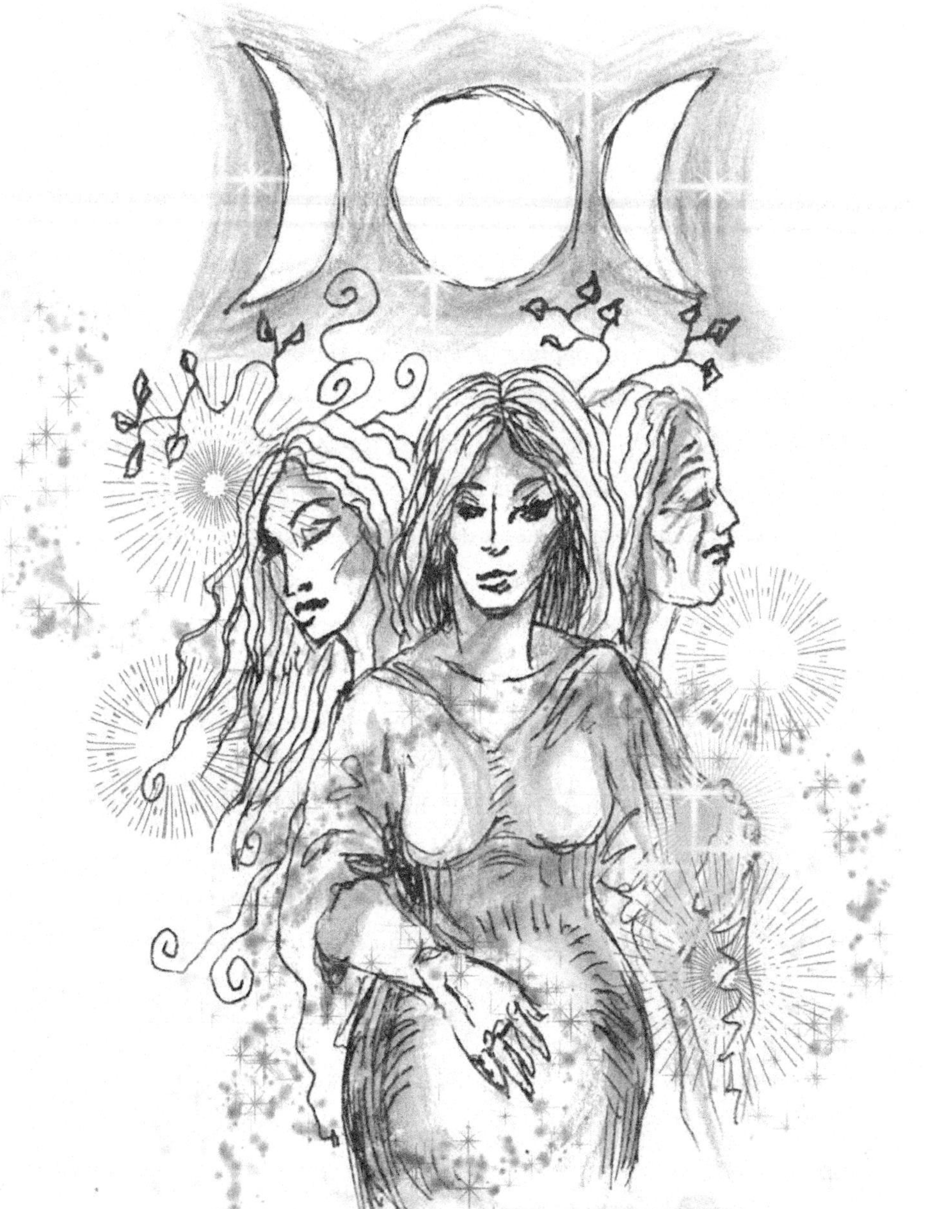

had entered the hut of the ancient crone. And of the strange things she had spoken to him there...

... He had been mesmerized by her hypnotic voice and the warmth of the fire. And how she had eventually fallen silent, but he remained in a trance for an indefinable time. It was interrupted, however, by an awareness of heat; the small fire was growing. The flames steadily increased, until they leapt up to the roof.

Oisin now smiled to himself as he reminisced how, like a fool, he had jumped up fearing it would set the hut alight. The brightness of the flames was dazzling and soon it was like looking into the midday Sun; the whole hut was filled with the intensity of the light.

He had looked this way and that, looking for the way out, fearing for his life. No less, when he saw strange figures moving within the flames... However, before long, the flames died down again and soon returned to their original intensity. As his eyes had grown accustomed to dim light again, he could see across the fire, the shadowy forms of three women. They seemed to be glowing with their own light.

As he watched spellbound, the three forms merged into one, leaving before him a beautiful young woman, naked in the firelight.

From the start. Oisin knew her to be Olwen - the Goddess of love.

More yellow was her long hair than the flowers of the broom,
Her skin whiter than the foam of the wave.
The eye of the bold Hawk,
The glance of a falcon was not brighter than hers.
Her bosom was more snowy than the breast of the white swan,
Her cheeks redder than the wild rose.
Her countenance was brighter than the blossom of the wood anemone
Amidst the spray of the meadow fountain.

Instantly he was filled with love for her - he could not move, but only stood there gawking and shaking like a new fold. For until then, the youth had never experienced a woman; he was innocent. She came over to the boy and led him to a collection of furs at the back of the Hut; and prepared him for his initiation into manhood.

There, she slowly undressed him. Encouraged him. And for the remainder of the night, taught him how to unlock the power and passion in a woman, the secret ways of love and ecstasy.

As their bodies and minds had merged as one, for a while, at least, he had known the mind of a woman. And came to realize his own gentle feminine nature, the creative, emotional, inspirational, and intuitive self.

For a brief moment, he knew what it was to be a whole person - a true man.

CHAPTER 9

Alder

It had rained once again during the night, rendering his rest time damp and miserable. However, as daylight emerged, the rain subsided and promised a dry day ahead. Oisin dismantled his camp and continued along the path. Amidst the silence of the forest, he became fixated on the towering trees that stood so still; they were colossal. Dark and overwhelming, they loomed over him like castles with their high-reaching branches pressing down on him.

He had never witnessed such grandeur in trees before. In his region of origin, most of the trees had been cleared out, leaving behind only smaller woodlands and coppiced areas. However, as he walked through this unfamiliar territory, a strange distortion occurred. He could only see a few yards of track at any given time. Beyond the trees barred his way, and on every side, into depth upon depth of green shadow. But as he walked again, the trees seemed to move aside to let him pass, then closed again behind him.

After some time, however, Oisin began to get used to this peculiar distortion effect. He passed through large stretches of great gnarled oaks; in other parts of this forest, yew flourished. While in yet another section, alder dominated. But it was clear that the mighty ash rose above them all.

The day progressed without much event until eventually, off in the distance came the sound of rushing water, further down the trail.

As he continued walking, the sound of the river grew louder. The trees thinned out as he approached an area where smaller bushes consisting mainly of alder, willow, and blackthorn replaced larger trees.

Eventually, he came upon the river. Its flowing waters, a raging turret swollen by recent days' rainfall. The bubbling waters roared past creating swirling eddies of yellow foam. The torrent tore great snatches of grass and clay out of the banks as it passed.

Across the other side, Oisin could clearly see the track continuing into the forest, but at the moment it was impossible to cross the water. It could take days to walk upriver to find a narrow crossing, but there seemed no other choice. Resigned to his fate, Oisin set off upstream. At dusk, he had made camp beside the river's relentless flow.

The next morning, Oisin awoke to a beautiful summer day. After drinking from the river, he continued his journey. It was almost mid-summer now, and the sun was approaching its zenith.

However, leaving the main track and trekking across country, somehow improved his humour. He felt happy and light, and he enjoyed very much the company of the river and its changing moods.

An adjoining stream, in a deep ravine had forced him back into the forest away from the raging river. It was quieter here and towards mid-morning, he gradually became aware of a faint sound, something like birdsong but wasn't. But then he began to realize it was the sound of someone playing pipes; he knew he had heard this music before! Its haunting melody drifted through the woodland, rising and falling, sometimes quick, sometimes slow, and melancholy.

He had stopped now to listen for a while. It was so beautiful, always so distant, and so quiet. Sometimes it was so quiet he couldn't hear it at all; he could just feel it, out there, calling him. It had a delicious mystery about it, haunting, and enticing him to discover its source. He knew he wanted to discover its source; he knew he would not regret it if he did.

As he listened, his mind started to wander; he could feel himself rising and falling with the sound of the pipes. Slowly, images formed in his mind blurred at first, but then he started to recognize it.

... A wide expanse of reeds and bulrushes, small lakes and marshy ground. The flat marshland stretched in all directions... Misty patches lay low and clung to the land. It looked like a wide sea of misty clouds, the whole scene had an ethereal, unearthly feel to it. In his vision, the mist cleared, revealing a lush, fertile island covered by apple orchards. In the very centre, was a small conical hill. Then a realisation came over him that this was where he needed to go... with that realisation, the vision slowly faded along with the music of the pipes...

He awoke to find himself back in the forest. Still a little dazed, he shook his head to clear his mind; now at least he knew where he needed to go. But which direction now? He had no idea. But with no other choice, he returned to the raging river, following it upstream.

After some time, he notices up ahead a large Alder tree standing before him. In it, a jet-black Raven is flitting from branch to branch; it seems to be trying to attract his attention. Now the raven had stopped and it turned its head knowingly. Seeing that Oisin had noticed, it flew on ahead a little. Oisin, on a whim, decides to follow this cheeky bird, 'maybe it will lead me to the magical island.' he thinks jokingly.

The Raven continues to lead him away from the river, acting as a guide. It flew overhead, scouting new paths but ever leading him deeper and deeper into the forest. And Oisin hopes, ever closer towards his destination, the mysterious island.

Bran the Raven teaches us how we can gain from the natural wisdom of the land and the trees. Our totem animals and other birds and animals can teach us much if only we take the time to study them. Looking at nature, and studying the way animals behave; much insight into basic human drives may be gained. The ancient Druids knew that nature was our greatest teacher. We can also gain many insights from flowing with music in all its forms. Music can take us many places in trance and teach us much if we let ourselves go and allow it to 'take' us.

For many days, Oisin travelled, following his new companion. He had named the bird 'Looks-far' as it flew high above him, acting as his guide to an unknown country. Like all tribesmen, he knew about which foods to collect and eat from the wild. He also encountered many wild animals in the forest, but so far none had bothered him. However, occasionally in the distance he heard the bellow of a wild stag, and he had the feeling that for some reason it was following him.

As he proceeded on his journey, the forest vegetation gradually changed and the ground became wet and boggy. Now he had to weave his way around patches of marshy ground, progress became increasingly more difficult. Eventually, though, the last of the trees gave way to a vast expanse of rushes that spread before him like a lush green sea. Patches of deeper water can be seen, but far in the distance, rising above the marsh lake is an island of firm ground; the very island he saw in his vision!

But how does he get there through the dangerous marsh? Oisin stood there bewildered for a moment until the familiar sound of Looks-Far caught his attention. Over to his right, the raven was flitting about beneath some bushes. Puzzled Oisin walked over to the bird, but it scampered under a bush. Shrugging his shoulders, Oisin crawls under the bush to follow. On the other side, he is just in time to see the bird disappearing into the reed bed. Again, Oisin follows. Now before him stretches a small causeway of Alder logs laid on marshland. His guide has helped him find his path to the island!

Oisin followed the secret path across the marsh for many miles. The sun was blisteringly hot now, for it was nearly mid-summer. With sweat dripping down his back, Oisin was beginning to feel uncomfortable. But at last, the land started rising out of the marsh.

Now he stood at the base of the conical hill. Before him, there is a path that leads past a small, pointed marker stone. A little further on, he comes across a spring bubbling out of the hillside into a small pool of crystal-clear water. Hot and sweating, Oisin is attracted to this inviting sight and quickly strides to its edge.

Stooping down, he cups his hands and takes a drink of the water; it is so cool and refreshing. But Oisin is still hot and sticky with sweat, so decides to plunge beneath the cool waters, bathing in the living waters of life. He holds his breath for a long time enjoying the coolness of the water. Eventually rising to the surface gasping, breathing in the fresh life-giving air, feeling exhilarated.

After a little while, he emerges from the pool and lays on the lush grass, feeling the Earth beneath him, healing and nurturing. Relaxing now, he feels the sun shine down onto his body, warming him and drying his skin. The warmth feels so good and life-giving.

As he lies there contented and half-asleep, he listens to the sound of the waters gurgling and spurting from the hillside. Within the sound, he fancies, he can hear faint voices, laughing and bubbling voices:

... They talk of 'living waters', of the lifeblood of Mother Earth, issuing forth from deep within her. They talk, too of the beneficial and healing qualities of this water, when drunk straight from the spring... And how it is very different from the trapped, dead water in pipes, tanks and bottles.

Oisin listens to the bubbling, babbling voices... They speak of a time in the future... A time when people will become so detached from nature and their own bodies and senses. That they will drink only chemically treated, 'dead' water from taps or bottles... And how they will grow to distrust the living waters of nature. Because they know, deep down, that people like themselves have polluted the land, the air, and the rivers. And they will know deep down that this is a great crime that is being committed...

CHAPTER 10

Ash

He awoke suddenly and found himself lying next to the spring. The babbling waters seemed to have stopped talking now, so Oisin raised himself to his feet and continued climbing the sacred mound. The path seemed to lead a snaking, spiralling path around the conical hill. He soon realized that this was a ceremonial pathway and that he was following a three-dimensional labyrinth pattern up the sacred Tor.

As Oisin reached the top of the sacred mound, he was greeted by a breathtaking view of the surrounding landscape. He felt a sense of peace wash over him as he surveyed the lush greenery of the marshes that stretched out before him. In the far distant horizon, he could just make out rolling hills.

Sitting down to rest and reflect on his journey so far, he thought back on all the challenges he had faced. Realising that each one had taught him something valuable about himself and the world around him. He had grown in ways he never thought possible, both physically and mentally.

But as he pondered the purpose of his quest, Oisin couldn't help but feel a sense of uncertainty. Was there truly a greater meaning to all of this? Or was it just a series of events leading him nowhere in particular?

Despite his doubts, Oisin knew that he couldn't give up now. He had come too far to turn back. With renewed determination, he stood up and looked about the small plateau at the top of the hill. There was little to see except a small, simple, unimpressive temple, of uncut stone.

Cautiously, he walks to the entrance. Each side of the doorway is a carved serpent, which snakes up the sides and then twists together around a spear above the doorway. The heavy oak door has been left open, so Oisin peers through the gloomy atmosphere into the temple; there is a strong smell of frankincense. As his eyes grew accustomed to the dim light, he could see a circular hearth. The stones contain a small fire. Beside it, sitting cross-legged is a holy man, eyes closed, deep in contemplation.

There is a profound silence within the temple; somehow Oisin is reluctant to enter, not wanting to disturb the peace of the place. But having come thus far, he draws up courage and quietly takes a step through the doorway

The Mage immediately opens his eyes saying, "Greetings my son I have been waiting a long time for you. Welcome to the temple of the eternal flame, dedicated to 'Lugh the Lord of shining light'. I have enjoyed watching your progress so far."

The Mage then gestures for Oisin to sit across from him. Awkwardly, Oisin complies, squatting beside the fireplace.

"For half a year the Sun King has grown," the Mage continued without preamble. "And now you are at your physical peak - you're prime. But soon your power will start to diminish. Up until now, you have relied purely on your strength and your skill. You have developed strength of character and your outward nature is shining brightly in the world. Now... Now, you must learn to acknowledge your waning energy and access your inner strength and your darker nature. It is imperative you learn to acknowledge this and know how to use it, or it will find its own way to manifest."

The Mage continued to teach Oisin. He spoke of how too much reliance on inner strength can lead to darkness and negativity. While too much focus on outer strength can lead to arrogance and a lack of humility. The key, he explained, is to find a balance between the two, acknowledging both the light and the dark within oneself. This lesson applies not just to your physical abilities but also to your emotional and spiritual growth, too.

Oisin listens intently but is confused. Then decries, "Sir, I am not all that you say." Oisin took a deep breath and continued, "At one time I was confident and knew my place in the tribe. But now in the Great Forest, I am full of doubts about myself and feel ignorant of the ways of the world. I can see no reason why I have been placed here; I feel that all seems to be without plan or meaning. As soon as I see one, it melts away into nothing, or into some other plan that I never thought possible. What before seemed central, suddenly becomes the rim, till I doubt that there was any shape or pattern. I am left to think it was never more than a trick of my mind, some false hope because my eyes and mind are tired from too much looking."

"Ah, my son," crooned the Mage benevolently. "What you have been trying to comprehend is the 'Great Plan', the 'Tao' the 'Great Dance of Shiva', which others call the 'Web of life' or the 'Wyrde'. It is simply: 'the universal dance of nature.' It is and always has been perfect. It is my duty to tell you more of these things."

The Mage settled down into a storyteller's cadence, while Oisin stared into the fire before him. "Some with weak and dark minds would put themselves apart from it, standing as if it were on the outside. Sometimes they peer through a tiny crack in the curtain, like small children not comprehending what they see. But we, all of us dance the Great Dance. The dance, which we dance is at the centre, and for the dance, all things were made. From the greatest galaxy to the tiniest speck of dust, hear in dwells the Great Spirit. The Great Spirit dwells within the seed of the smallest flower and is not cramped. Yet the whole universe is inside him, and he is not stretched.

"You are a perfect being of the humankind. Although your race appears to rule the earth, and it was for you that it was made, the worlds are for themselves. The sea you have never seen, the fruit you have never harvested, the fire through which your bodies can not pass. Even the mountains you cannot climb, do not wait for your coming, to be perfect; yet they will rejoice when you come. The countless years before man came were not a desert. Nature has its voice- she is also at the centre." While speaking this last, the Mage seemed to grow in size, filling the temple. His voice had increased to a booming crescendo, which echoed from the very walls of the temple. Oisin became afraid.

Pausing for a moment, the holy man continued with more compassion. "Little one, be comforted that man's voice is not the only voice. There are many places on earth that man still hasn't been to. Yet it is not for nothing that the Great Spirit laboured to create them. All things have their place in the Great Dance."

Oisin had been trying to understand, and was still a little afraid of the powerful Mage, now bemoaned, "But where do I fit into all this?"

The Mage looked over at Oisin with kindly eyes, yet there was pity there too as he spoke. "Man, too has his place at the centre, yet he is not central as some of your kind see it. A great temple may have a priest and a janitor, both are essential to the running of the temple. And it was created for them, as it was created for all. But they do not own it, it is for all to be in; so too is the Earth. Each grain is at the centre, the dust is at the centre, and the planets are at the centre. Each beast and plant is at the centre. The Gods and Goddesses are there also.

"The Great Spirit is everywhere. All of him is in everything. Each thing was made for him, and he is at the centre. And because the Great Spirit is within us, each of us is at the centre."

The Mage paused for a moment and shifted his position slightly. His eyes became sad as he began again in a harsher voice. "It is not this way in the cities of the darkened world. Here they say that each must live for all, when in reality each is working for the benefit of the few. In the plan of the Great Dance, plans without number interlock. Each movement becomes in its season the breaking into flower of the whole design to which all else has been directed. Each thing is infinitely necessary but also infinitely superfluous. Your love for life and the world shall be like this, born neither of your need, nor deserving, but a plain bounty.

"Only to the darkened mind does all seem aimless and without plan, because there are more plans than it looked for. The Wyrde, the Web, the tapestry of life, is woven so closely, with fibres so fine. That unless a man looked long and closely at them, he would see neither threads nor weaving at all, but only see the same and the flat."

Oisin, shaking his head in frustration, blurted, "But I still don't understand. What exactly do, I, need to do?"

The wise Mage answered, "In the Great Dance, set your eyes on one thread, it will lead you through all patterns. And it will seem to you the master movement. But this seaming will be true; let non say otherwise. This is the secret that the ancient Druids passed down to us; the secret is woven in the Celtic Knots". He paused again while Oisin continued staring into the flames.

The sage put another log on the fire, and after it caught alight, Oisin could see vivid images of the Great Dance. It was an infinitely complex Celtic knot design, woven out of intertwining, undulating cords of light of every colour. They leapt over and under each other in an impossible intricacy. Oisin could recognise figures of animals and fish within the design. There were birds and humans, too. As he looked at each figure, it became the principal figure and the focus of the whole design. But then, as he looked more closely at each detail, more would be revealed. Drawing him deeper and deeper into a fractal pattern, constantly repeating, yet infinitely variable, never the same.

Yet each part seemed to contain and reflect the whole design in a three-dimensional hologram. Yet again, at the same time, it was somehow made clear to him that the pattern spanned more than three dimensions, though how many he could not say.

Then gradually the focus of the design became disentangled, and it was clear that it was only part of a mere marginal decoration. Yet its significance was not diminished at all but added to the richness of the whole pattern.

How long Oisin sat there in a trance looking at the images that unfolded before him, he could not say. It seemed to him so much, it could have been days, weeks even. He only knew that when he finally became aware of his body again and found himself still seated before the eternal fire. The sun had set and there was darkness outside the temple. But he was left with an unmistakable feeling that he should seek out the centre. The centre of the Great Forest.

Across the fire, the Mage seemed asleep. But the moment Oisin looked upon him, his eyes sprang open. He sat up saying, "I have contemplated long your journey so far. Now you begin a new one, different from before. To align with this, from now on you will be known as Kesh".

Without another word, the sage put his hand down to the hearth and onto a long pair of blacksmith tongs, which he had not noticed before. With them, the wise Mage moved the glowing embers to one side. Then plunged into the heart of the fire, removing a glowing, white-hot spearhead.

Nimbly, the Mage took it to a vat of thick black oil, by the wall and quickly lunged the spearhead into the oil. Flames, sparks, and thick oily smoke belched from the vat. After a little while, the smoke cleared, and Kesh could see the Mage cleaning the spearhead on a piece of sacking. When he was satisfied, the Mage brought the spearhead over to Kesh.

"Here is the magical spear of Lugh," he said, "Mount it on your staff, for this is the tool you will need for the rest of your journey. Guard it well for it is your 'Excalibur', it has the power to find your truth, your 'destiny'. For it is also called the 'Spear of Destiny'. Now I have spoken enough, it is time for action. Leave now my son, go find your destiny - your truth."

The Ash represents the need for strength and control in life on all levels; macrocosm and microcosm. Where the individual is in command of their situation and must act accordingly even in the face of adversity. Ash is doing and directing action on a physical level. It represents the warrior in their prime. One who has developed skills and is ready to face what life has to offer. They are ready for the quest for the Holy Grail – for TRUTH - for Excalibur. They are searching for their place in life, and how they are a part of - and linked to the Greater Whole. Understanding this will enhance your understanding of smaller everyday problems.

CHAPTER 11

Rowan

It had been in the dead of night when he left the temple. Trying to go downhill in the dark would be foolhardy, so he had decided to rest awhile till the first light of dawn. He found a hidden valley on the eastern side of the sacred hill and tried to sleep.

He was awoken as the dawning sun shone its first rays onto his face. Blinking in the light, he found he had been lying near a jumble of stones that looked to be the remains of an old cottage.

However, as he approached the stones, a strange sight suddenly struck him. There stood a beautiful Rowan tree, but it was growing out of the remains of an old apple tree, one tree on top of another. The cheerful red berries shone so brightly in the morning sunshine that it looked like a thousand burning red coals. Struck by the grace and beauty of this tree, he could not help but go over to touch its bark. He could not help himself as he embraced the tree; basking in its Fay energy.

To the people of his tribe, this tree was the embodiment of the fire and sky Goddess Brigit; he had grown to love her. To his teacher and mentor, the old Shaman, the tree was especially revered. Many times, he had credited this tree with the inspiration he had received at difficult times.

Kesh embraced the tree as a man might embrace a lover. As he did so, he realized there was a deep-rooted need in him for the compassion and love of a woman. The thought saddened him, that soon he would have to leave this tree and his feelings behind.

As he fondly surveyed the tree, he noticed that one of the dead branches, just above him was unusually shaped. It was knobbly and twisted, and an old knot had shrunk and fallen out, leaving a hole through the branch. Using his inner sight, as the old shaman had taught him, he could see within the curves of the wood, the shape of a reclining Goddess. Further down, the wood had split and now looked like a pair of legs. Taking hold of it, it easily came away from the tree.

Sitting down at the base of the tree with his 'gift', he was inspired to carve it. So he began to carve with a flint knife he had made during his travels. After only a small amount of work, he had accentuated what was already there and carved a beautiful goddess into the wood. Truly a gift of a goddess figurine from the goddess tree.

> *Though I am old with wandering*
> *Through hollow lands and hilly lands,*
> *I will find out where she has gone,*
> *And kiss her lips and take her hands;*
> *And walk among the long dappled grass,*
> *And pluck till time and times are done*
> *The silver apples of the moon,*
> *The golden apples of the Sun.*
>
> W.B. Yeats

He had been taught to respect the power of protection such figures gave, especially if carved from Rowan wood. He thought he would certainly need this on the journey to come. After giving thanks to the Goddess and the tree, he set off walking again, well pleased.

It had grown into a beautiful day; the sun was beating down. After some time, Kesh found himself wandering through a series of apple orchards with lush green trees and fruit heavy on the branches. With such abundance among the trees, the humidity was high, creating a hazy atmosphere with dandelion seeds and bees filling the air. It felt like paradise, idyllic and soon he began to feel too hot to travel; the heat made him lazy, and he was really thirsty.

Suddenly he came to an abrupt halt; he had almost walked into a figure standing directly in his path. Kesh was startled. He hadn't seen her coming. She just seemed to appear in front of him.

The fair maiden was dressed in shadowy gauze-like robes, which seemed to ruffle when there was no wind. She was tiny, only four feet tall, and very young but had pure white hair flowing down her back. She had an unusually, chiselled but stunningly attractive face with very high cheekbones. Her ears came to a point at the top, and she had penetrating pink eyes that held his gaze.

"Why do you travel so earnestly Sir, when it is so hot? Here, why not stay a while and refresh yourself." She held up a clay flagon of cider.

Kesh still hadn't recovered from the surprise of her sudden appearance. But cautiously he accepted the cider; for he was very thirsty. Hungrily glugging it down, he found it certainly was delicious and very refreshing.

"Here, sit and rest and I will rub your tired shoulders," crooned the Fay maiden.

Gratefully, Kesh accepted the offer. Long had he travelled on his quest and needed to relax and be healed. The Fay maiden skilfully massaged his back and shoulders. Kesh quickly let himself relax and felt himself melting into the soft earth beneath him. The Fay maiden smiled to herself and continued massaging.

"I can tell by your standing that you are a warrior on a quest. I am curious; tell me, what is it you quest for so earnestly?"

Dreamily, and half-absently, Kesh replied, "My truth."

"And where is this truth?" Quizzed the maiden.

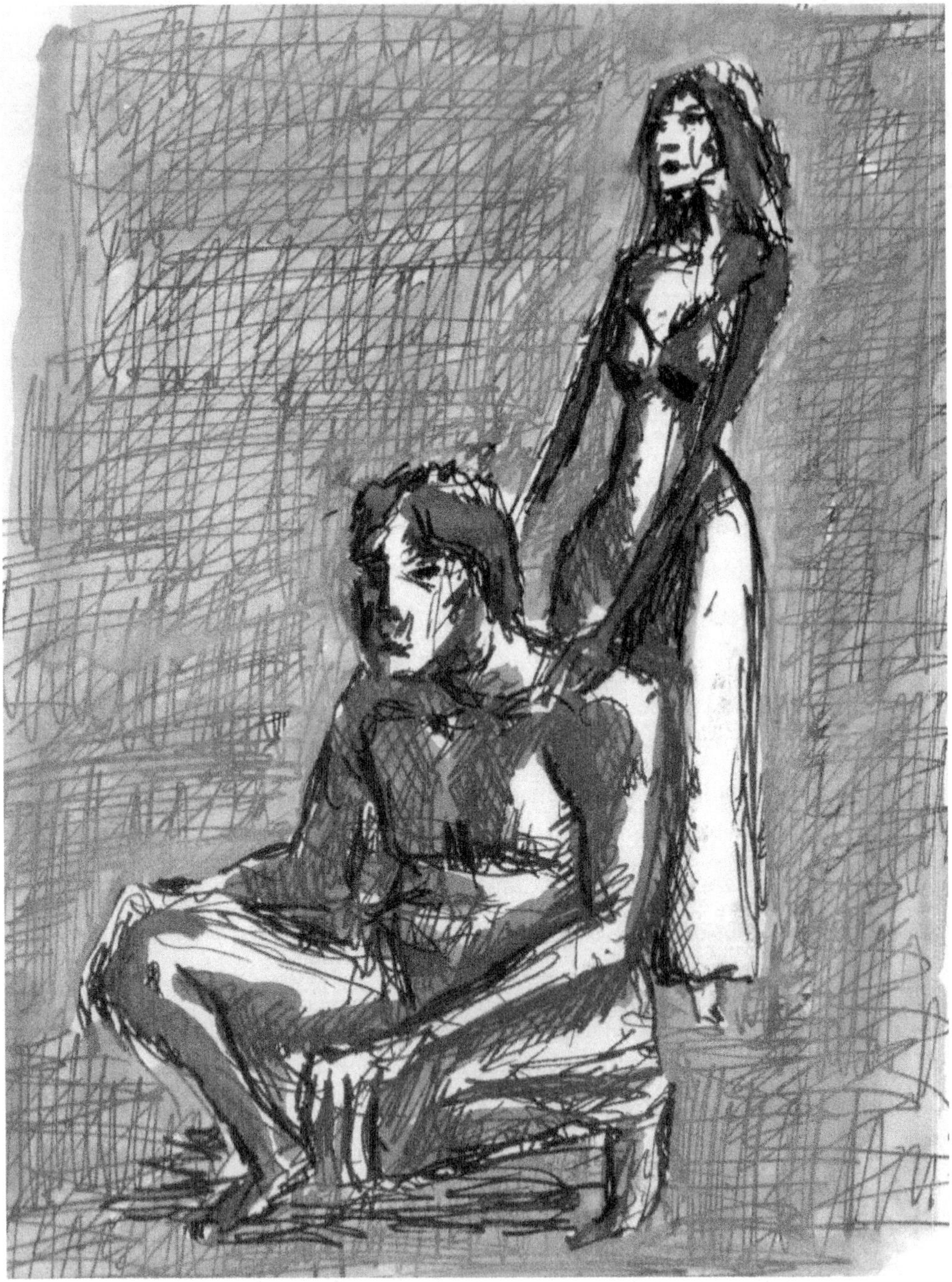

"At the centre of the forest," replied Kesh, now half asleep.

The Fay maiden finished her massage and sat on a nearby log. Kesh stretched lazily on the ground. How weary he was of travelling and questing. Lying here in this idyllic setting, with this beautiful maiden beside him. His mind began to think of home and how he missed his family and friends. He knew many of his friends would have found partners by now and have their own hearth fire and all the comforts of a home.

"Why look you so sad, young Sir?" quizzed the Fay maiden seductively.

"I am thinking of my home and friends, I miss them so."

"Why seek 'truth' at the centre of the forest, when surely the only truth is your home and family, and maybe by now, a wife awaits you there."

Kesh suddenly sat up, "Yes! 'Tis true, why do I quest to become a god when I could have all those mortal pleasures." With a look of purpose, he stood up. "I have quested enough; I will return home." Kesh immediately started to leave but then remembered the maiden.

"Fair maiden, you have done me well this day, but I have nothing to repay you with. But wait yes, I have my carving." Taking the figurine from his tunic, he quickly placed it in the hands of the Fay maiden, before she could refuse. But too late, with a horrifying screech, she exclaims, "No! No! No!"

Before Kesh's bewildered eyes, she contorted and quivered, shrieking like a Banshee. In disbelief he watches her wither away before his very eyes, reducing her down to nothing but a small heap of mouldering apples. In disgust, he watches the writhing maggots crawl out and fall to the ground.

"What sorcery is this?" Kesh cries out in amazement. "Some deception to stray me from my path." He quickly reclaimed his carving, rubbing it clean.

With only one backward glance, he continued on his quest.

Rowan reminds us to hold true to our highest ideals,
Standing firm and true as the warrior,
Safeguarding against malicious influences.

But still, as he wandered, Kesh couldn't help but think, there was much truth in the words of the Fay trickster...

CHAPTER 12

Birch

Kesh had spent the night beside a small lake. It was situated on higher ground and was dotted about with silver birch trees. He had risen early and was now famished. Searching about, he found some mushrooms under the birch trees and gathered some for his breakfast. They were a strange sort, red with white dots, but he had seen the old shaman gathering them often and figured they must be good to eat.

However, he was disappointed, but they satisfied his hunger. Packing his skin bag with his flint knife and fire-making stones he had gathered along the way; he took up his staff and was ready to journey once again.

He was striding along but still wasn't sure about which direction he should go. Soon, he re-entered the forest, and as before, it stretched out as far as he could see in every direction. Before long, however, his thoughts returned to how easily he had been seduced by the Fay maiden. But, he reassured himself, he had overcome the distraction using the power of the Goddess. And after, he saw it as a distraction and recommitted to his quest.

Yes, this quest had changed him. He now realized that he had started this journey half-hearted, almost reluctant. His old self had felt that it was something thrust upon him, against his will. He had felt like a victim, 'Why was this happening to me?' He had thought, 'Why not somebody more worthy, somebody who wanted to go on this quest?'

Now he was feeling more positive about the whole adventure. In fact, he felt really good now - euphoric. This seemed to be reflected in the very landscape about him. The trees looked somehow greener with a surreal vividness. Above him, the bright sunlight cast a dappled light through the branches, as they swung to and fro in the wind. They seemed to sway in a crazy dance of their own, to the rhythm of the wind; the effect caused a strange stroboscopic light.

But it was all too bright for his eyes. Closing them until they were small slits, the effect caused a world full of blurred colour and light and rainbows.

A sensual ecstasy flows over his body, which feels lighter, giving him a sensation of floating. This is heightened by the appearance of the clouds, which seem to race towards him. They take on the appearance of fantastic animals; a horse with a twisting spiralling tail; a wild boar full of spirally patterns; a strange dog with hackles raised and red ears; a dragon whose body twists this way and that, as a sudden up-draught blusters the vapours.

Suddenly he is in the clouds. A world of white noise and white light all about him. An awareness flows over him of some sort of indefinable presence. Of infinitely many, yet all of one. A feeling of great love and warmth and welcome. A sense of at last 'coming home', of 'belonging'. Kesh basks in this for what seems like an indeterminate time.

Unexpectedly, his whole body experiences a sudden rush, an exhilarating sense of falling. Now he can see the landscape below him. A patchwork of small fields with animals grazing in some of them. He can see spiralling patterns of telluric energy flowing in the land. Some of the animals are lying in the centre of these energy spirals, contentedly chewing. They seem to sense some benefit or good feeling from an unknown source. Concentric rings of energy radiate from small beacon hills where the 'bone' fires are lit during festival times.

Now he saw great lichen-covered stones, carved with ancient Ogham signs, that some call Menhirs. They point to the sky and seem to radiate complex spiralling energy patterns. While another energy of white light seems to connect stones with hilltops and wells, in a straight line. Yet this, in turn, is part of a greater grid pattern, a spider's web of light spreading across the entire countryside.

Another dream-like awareness washes over him. He somehow feels the presence of something very special and beautiful. He knows it to be the fertile essence of nature, the very spirit of the earth. The pregnant, birthing Earth Mother. She, in whose honour the birch poles would be erected, and decorated with ribbons and danced about. Couples would pair off and celebrate their fertile nature, in the surrounding fields. Lost in Tantric bliss, all in Her name.

Now Kesh could see Her form in the very landscape below him. Her pregnant belly and breasts are the rounded hills. Her hair, the forest canopy. Two small blue lakes become Her eyes. A gentle wind passing through Her forest hair seems to lovingly fondle Her abundant foliage. A soft rain now falls on Her round hill breasts, seeming to caress them as they gather together in little gullies.

Flowing fingers of water pass down Her pregnant belly. Some of it entered tiny crevices in Her body, following hidden passageways deep into the womb of the earth. Now a spring bursts forth from the hillside from a place that becomes Her sacred Yoni, giving birth to the waters of life.

If we look closely, we can see all Her features.
She gives selflessly of her body to feed the children of the Earth.
She asks for nothing in return.

Kesh is left with a feeling of wonder and awe at his vision. And a definite 'knowing' that he is now embarking upon the most challenging part of his adventure. That of entering the Dream-Time of the underworld.

As Kesh gradually descends onto the forest floor again. Slightly relieved he finds himself lying on a soft bed of moss; gradually he starts becoming aware of his own body again. However, this awareness makes him realise he is now feeling very nauseous. He retches and vomits several times.

After a while, his body starts to feel better. Now, of course, he realized how foolish he had been and how childish those previous negative thoughts had been. He knew now that sometimes the gods had an agenda that we humans may not comprehend. From time to time, we may receive tiny glimpses of a small part of the pattern. But we can never comprehend the greater picture. Why was he questioning their will? Who was he to question who the 'chosen one' should be? He should be honoured, damn it!

Gradually, he started feeling honoured in his own way. And proud to be chosen, no matter how unworthy he felt. Perhaps this, was part of the reason for choosing? This was his Vision Quest; he had now taken it on board; he owned it. It was part of him, as much as he was a part of it.

With this new resolution in his heart, Kesh strides on with renewed vigour. New strength derived from a fresh sense of purpose and resolve. At last, he feels that he has a definite goal to aim for and the knowledge that his goal is in sight. A cool breeze blows in his face, refreshing him.

Yes, this is a new beginning for him, a fresh start - a second wind. He has put behind him all those doubts and fears that were holding him back and entering a new phase in his journey. And with a definite resolve, that from now on he will be very particular about what he breakfasts upon.

CHAPTER 13

Yew

Kesh had been walking for many days now. However, in the Great Forest, time seemed to have no meaning. Kesh thought that it had been several days since the revealing visions induced by the teacher plants - the shaman's mushroom. But equally, it could have been several weeks.

His sleep had been fitful lately. He dreamt of hidden presences that remained just out of sight; yet somehow he was fully cognizant of their presence. He didn't like what he saw, either. Also, he sensed a disturbance deep within his soul and was aware of several imminent changes coming over him. It felt as if someone had stirred up the bottom of a well. Causing the muddy waters at the core of his being to bubble up into his daily consciousness.

At times when he lay half asleep, he would hear the reedy pipe music - he had heard it many times now along this journey. But now, somehow, it seemed more persistent, almost taunting him. But each time Kesh woke up, there was no sign or trace of this music whatsoever.

Wearily, he rose from his slumber, feeling compelled to press on, for he was becoming increasingly aware that the forest's centre was drawing near.

He continued westward. After several miles, he realised he had not seen any animals or heard any birdsong in quite some time. So stops for a moment to listen, but there is only an uncanny silence all around him. The eerie atmosphere pervades his consciousness, causing him to be overcome with a growing uneasiness.

More cautious now, he continues westward. The sun was sinking low in the sky now, and through the trees the setting sun blinded him with its piercing rays, impeding his progress. Nevertheless, after some time, he arrives at a pathway flanked by two rows of Yew trees that stretches ahead for over a mile. 'Clearly', Kesh thought, 'this ceremonial walkway leads somewhere important'. But despite having misgivings about what awaited him at the end of it, Kesh continued along the walkway.

After some way, he became aware of a low murmuring, like that of many voices talking together in the next room. The murmuring gradually grew louder as he walked. Now he was sure he could see a large structure visible at the very end of the walkway. But the sun was almost set and shining directly behind it, making it difficult for him to see clearly.

The ominous murmuring was getting much louder now. Up ahead, the sunlight blinded him - each step became more challenging than the last. The blinding sunlight seemed to be coming from every direction now; the murmuring was impossibly loud. His head began to spin, inducing a dizzying sensation.

Kesh feels compelled to continue making progress, but can only stagger slowly forward before finally collapsing to his knees. He covered his ears with his hands and lowered his aching head to the ground to blank out the dazzling light.

He remains like this for some time, gasping for breath with his face pressed against the earth. Suddenly, cracks begin to form in the ground beneath him and a brilliant light emanates from within them. In awe and with bleary eyes, he peers through the fissures only to find himself staring incredulously at another world unfolding before him...

... A small village in a wooded area, little children playing happily in the river. Kesh gasps as he realizes it is his village. He can see himself as a small boy playing with the others... nearby a young man chopping wood; and a village woman picking fruit in the woods.

The scene changes... now a large metallic monster machine grabs hold of the sacred trees and rips them out of the ground... strange men with torches set fire to the bushes... forest animals are fleeing in terror.

... Now huge chimneys discharge black smoke into the pure air... factories belch out poisons into crystal clear rivers, till they run red or white or grey... Kesh stares in disbelief, "Surely this could not be... people would never do this... could never forget."

... The scene changes again... A huge explosion of unbelievable power creates a mushroom cloud... The ground was left burnt and scorched, thousands of people and animals lying dead... People blinded are stumbling over the charred bodies.

... In another city, an angry man breaks down a door... beats a terrified woman with a long stick, then wrecks her house, stealing nothing! ... Three young boys push an old woman into the gutter, kicking her poor body, then steal money from her purse... "No... No... No... this cannot be... no one would... to a wise one?"

The scene changes again... a sunny day in a pleasant modern city park, a young pregnant woman is walking happily, with her four-year-old daughter... Suddenly a man jumps out and drags her into the bushes, beats and kicks her, then rapes her... as the small child looks on in disbelief...

"No... No... these are lies," Kesh sobs in disbelief. "This could never be true... to dishonour the Mother so... "

Horrified, Kesh jumps up, covering his eyes as he blindly runs back down the path screaming "No... no..."

But he trips over a twisted root, landing flat down on the ground again. Now he tries to get back up. His passionate eyes searched this way and that for a way out of this nightmare. But looking back down the path stops him in his tracks... Kesh stares in horror. Each of the Yew trees he passed earlier, now has a bleached skull mounted on the back; death stares him in the face.

He cannot go back. He cannot go on. In dismay, Kesh buries his face in his arms and weeps and weeps like a child; till gradually a deep and troubled sleep overtakes him.

Sometime later, he is roused from his troubled slumber by a mellifluous voice, emanating from a very old woman. However, he discerns a profound sense of empathy in her tone. "Rest easy my child; you have come a long way in so short a time."

Kesh cautiously raises his head but is taken aback by what he beholds. Incredulously before him stands an exceedingly ancient Yew tree. Her gnarled and twisted arms spread out before her. Her skin is the colour of autumn leaves. Her moss-coloured hair hangs down over her body. An oval cleft in her trunk oozes reddish sap, which slowly trickles onto the earth below.

She stands seemingly unchanging, but every time he looks away, she appears to shimmer and change. Kesh recollects from the old tribal stories that she must be one of the arboreal beings. Some call her the 'Yew Mother' or Wudu-Maer; the ancient guardian of the forest and all its creatures.

Yew has a shrewd understanding of your present situation, and what is going on around you. She can draw upon the wisdom gained from your past lives. She is willing to bestow these qualities as a gift to you, allowing the wisdom and skills that were always there, to be remembered. There may also be other gifts she is willing to give you, but as always with these things, you have to pay a price. In exchange for these gifts, you are expected to use them for the benefit of others. Like the sacrificial king or the birthing Earth mother - you have to give of yourself for the benefit of others.

The Yew Mother speaks again, "Human child, you have come so far on your chosen path and have been granted special talents and gifts that others do

Spirit Quest: The Heros Journey 75

not have. You have even journeyed to the awful gates of Hell and peered through the very cracks between the worlds. You were honoured to be granted visions of what is to come... and what may be... Yet, now you choose to turn your back on all this? "

Kesh hangs his head in shame but says nothing.

"The path you take is a one-way road," the Yew Mother continues. "You cannot come this far, then turn back... for if you do, you will stare into the very face of death itself. The road is lined with the skulls of those who have weakened and turned. This is no physical death... no, nothing so easy. But it will be the death of you as a person, the death of your very Soul."

Kesh, red-eyed answers, "But I cannot go on. Those things I saw... were so very terrible... surely these things cannot be?"

"Sadly those things will come to pass; people will forget the old ways, all too easily. However, the ancient mother is the ruler of life, death, and rebirth. You must remember the phoenix and how she burns her own nest, so as her young may rise out of the ashes... 'Tis the way things must be.

"The visions can be a burden. But to be fully alive is everything. You know the blessings of the sun intensely, likewise the cold of winter. You are alive to the Moon and Earth, to every magical vibration of stone and flower, stream and candle flame. You feel the pain of others, as well as your own. And so too the pain of the Earth as she is despoiled and abused. We walk a knife edge between great joy and great despair. 'Tis a burden all those on 'the path' face at some time. And in many ways, we pay heavily for 'the gifts' we receive. But such sorrows and pain, joys and ecstasy are ours and most would not have it any other way".

She shall teach things that are yet unknown; and ye shall dance, sing, feast, make music, and love, all in Her praise. For Hers is the ecstasy of the spirit and Hers also is joy on earth;
for Her law is love unto all beings. Keep pure your highest ideal; strive ever towards it; let nought stop you or turn you aside.
For Hers is the secret door which opens upon the land of youth and

Hers is the cup of wine of life, and the cauldron of Ceridwen; which is the Holy Grail of immortality. She is the gracious Goddess, who gives the gift of joy unto the heart of man.

Upon earth, she gave the knowledge of the spirit eternal; and beyond death, She gives peace and freedom, and reunion with those who have gone before. From Her all things proceed, and unto Her, all things must return.

Extract from the Charge of the Goddess

CHAPTER 14

W. Poplar

The prophetic visions had depleted Kesh, and his encounter with the Yew Mother had unsettled him. Nonetheless, he found solace in knowing that he was performing a timeless and sacred ritual. While alone in his actions, he was not alone in spirit.

As he proceeded along the Yew walkway, it now seemed less threatening. It still filled him with a sense of awe for the ceremonial walkway was ageless and magnificent. The branches of the ancient Yews bent down to the ground outside the walkway. Some had even taken root, creating something like another row outside the first.

The walkway was truly ageless. It gave off an impression that many, many before him had walked this very same path - alone, yet determined to undergo initiation. To get here, his journey had been long and convoluted; turning this way and that, like he was lost in a maze. Or more correctly, a labyrinth - for no matter which way he travelled, he knew that he was always getting nearer the centre.

The Yew Mother had taught him there was no turning back. This realization somehow made it easier for him to accept. No more grappling with conflicting emotions; instead, he focused solely on achieving the centre of the forest.

Now he had reached the final stretch of the walkway. He could see the centre of the Labyrinth - it took the form of a massive circular earthwork. It only remained to undertake that final challenge, not a physical barrier, but a psychological one.

Kesh stood motionless, gazing at the massive earthwork, the centre of the forest's labyrinth. As he stood still and silent, he could detect a faint hint of pipe music drifting on the breeze. And he realized that the thing that had been calling him in the forest all this time, was the reedy pipe music. This music stirred something deep inside all those who heard it. It was like facing a mirror - a reflection of one's soul. Although it evoked different emotions in each person. Kesh knew that some people may not hear the music at all. And yet others hearing it were afraid of the music. Fearing it so much that they would drown out its sweet notes with incessant chatter. Or seek out other noise, immersing themselves in the chaotic bustle of the big cities.

This secret, magical music represents one of the mysteries of life. Many have experienced this mystery, knowing it to be a masculine energy. They have personified it, giving it a name. Some call him Cernunnos or Mabon. The Teuton's called him Uller, the winter bowman. The Greeks and Romans knew him too but named different aspects Apollo, Orion, and Pan.

The Egyptians called him Amen-Ra, the Hindus Surya, and the Hebrews - Nimrod. Essentially, the mystery for some is a Solar God. For others, a huntsman and Lord of the Animals; a hunter but also the hunted.

It is a confusing mixture for some, but more recently in Britain, the Mystery became 'The Green Man'; 'Robin Goodfellow' or Robin Hood. Portrayed as a Fay trickster figure; for he plays with people by reflecting. He reflects what you bring to him, what is inside - but increases it three-fold.

If you come to him in fear, you may panic. If you come reverently, he may appear as a majestic stag or as the great god Pan - protector of forest animals. If you approach him with evil in your heart, you may find the demonic figure of Satan. If you approach him with lust, it may overtake you.

All the while Kesh had been dreaming, he had been walking; but unaware of it. For now, surprise overtook him, for he stood before the giant earthwork. He knew that such megalithic structures had been laid down by the old ones. Those that had come across the sea aeons ago, escaping their sinking lands.

This earthwork had a deep ditch or moat, surrounding a ring of earth some thirty feet high and easily a mile across. They had covered the circular earthwork with white chalk so that in the bright autumn sunshine it looked dazzling white.

Now to his right, he noticed a narrow gap in the earth ring. A massive oak tree had been felled and laid across the moat, creating a bridge. Deducing this must be the entrance, he mounts the fallen giant and passes through the earth ring. An incredible spectacle assaulted his senses.

Now, Kesh could see that the entire centre of the earthwork was a huge grove of white poplar trees. The bright sunshine and the wind blowing through the tree branches vibrated millions of leaves, creating a shimmering effect like sunlight on water. Millions of flecks of white light twinkling and flashing, the effect was quite astounding. But, at the same time, the sound of millions of leaves fluttering in the wind, created an almighty rushing, whispering sound; which filled his head.

A narrow pathway leads into the grove. So he followed the path through the grove towards the centre; all the while the shimmering lights and the whispering of the leaves stunned his senses. Unearthly and unreal sensations were filling his very being, and now he became less and less aware of his own body.

He has a rising sensation. He felt like he was leaving his body. And Kesh realises that he is now entering the timeless Dreamtime. He started to hear voices within the whispering leaves; some calling his name. He could recognise the voice of his tutor, the old Shaman. Now the voice of the Yew

Mother and the Green Man, all speaking at once. There were many other voices too, that he had encountered on his life's journey.

... "The longer I live, the more I realize that I'm just following my body. I just go with what my body is doing. It knows what to do. The thoughts that enter my mind are just a side effect, a by-product of my body's 'doing.' The mind with its ego and arrogance, fools itself it is in control."

..."The logical conclusion for my intellect would be to say that 'seeing' is bodily knowledge. The predominance of the visual sense in us influences this bodily knowledge and makes it seem eye-related"

On and on, the voices babble with often opposing and conflicting viewpoints. They seem to over-ride and overshadow each other, constantly vying for his attention, till his head is spinning.

Eventually, it all becomes too much to bear and he is overcome and forced to shout, "NO ...!" his voice deep and loud. "NO! NO! NOOoooooo...!"

Immediately, the whispering voices stop.

With a horrific jolt, he was in his body again - whole and strong. 'Instinct', he thought, 'It was his animal instincts that would help him now.'

Grabbing firmly onto his staff with both hands. He stood solid with his legs apart. Solid as a tree. His legs became the roots, growing deep into the ground searching for nutrients, searching for the empowering, healing Dragon energies of the earth. He was awakening the Dragon within himself. He could feel the energy drawing up his legs now. It was a slow sort of energy, quite different from the lightning bolt energy from the heavens. Green, it was, like a green snake coiling around his legs. Creeping, it was, creeping ever so slowly up his thighs. Oh, so slow - erotic and tantalizing, filling him with the smells of the forest. Bouquets of forest flowers, baskets full of ripe forest fruits, and the pungent but unmistakable smell of deer musk.

With that irresistible musky smell, he could feel his manhood throbbing. The fecundity and wildness of the Green Man flowed through him; his phallus was now hard and erect. But he realised quickly it wasn't sexual arousal, or at least not in the normal sense of the word. But more of a sense of wholeness, of completion.

For the first time, he knew what it felt like to be a whole man. Not the aggressive sort, but more the mystical warrior. It was a sense of knowing his function here on earth. To be the stout guardian and protector of all life on earth. The possessor of great courage and bravery, strength and willpower. He represented primal, male energy, the fecundity of the green man, the prime male fertilizer. With strength of purpose and the ability to overcome and survive... he would survive.

CHAPTER 15

Mistletoe -Heather

Kesh, stood solid as a tree, in the poplar grove at the very centre of the forest. He is lost in his visions, oblivious to the world. But suddenly, he is brought to his senses by the sound of a deafening bellow. His eyes flash open and he quickly turns in the direction of the noise.

A chilling sight greets him. Out of the trees struts a gigantic stag. Never before had he seen this beast's equal; it stood taller than a man, powerfully built with massive shoulders and haunch. Its head was broad and powerful and held on an immensely muscled neck. Atop his regal head sprouts a magnificent spread of antlers, a full ten feet across, proclaiming his might and power.

The giant stag regards him with a gleaming hostile eye. Kesh is rooted to the spot. The sheer wonder of the beast's majestic presence, its size, and its eerie silence, sent thrills of exquisite horror tingling along his spine. Kesh could feel the hairs on the back of his head stand on end and his mouth went dry.

The stag bellows another challenge, as it tears up the turf with a huge ringing hoof. Kesh somehow knows that before he can go any further, he must take on this challenge. The challenge of the Stag.

This is the biggest challenge for most men to overcome the desire to be 'The Stag', to rut among the females of the herd. That is not to say that all men do this. It may be only a secret desire or fantasy to be contained behind the 'safe' doors of the mind. But this is still a desire, regardless. It is no good simply masking this, saying, "Yes, I have overcome this now, and I am now an enlightened 'new age man'." This is dishonest and a delusion. What is needed is that you face the desire, head on, and honestly overcome the Stag.

For by overcoming the desire to be 'The Stag', you can 'become' the King Stag (and in so doing become the God Cernunnos).

This is not to say that you have to go out and cut off your balls; cease being a man. Like the ancient Greek priests of the goddess Cybele did, before her sacred altar. No, what is needed is that you learn to balance your male and female aspects. In this way, you become a 'True Man', a 'Rainbow Warrior', the mystical warrior, an enlightened 'person'; who is worthy to fertilize the eggs in the womb of the Goddess.

So Kesh, with his spear in his hand, battles long and hard with the giant stag. It is a magnificent battle. The stag with such majestic strength; the young man with skill and cunning.

However, eventually, Kesh manages to get on top of the stag, sitting astride its broad shoulders and holding on to the beast's huge antlers. Kesh manages to take control of the situation. The giant stag frantically rages, bucking about, until it is exhausted.

But just when Kesh thinks the stag is defeated, it falls to its knees on the ground. The beast suddenly thrusts its head back and flicks Kesh high over its antlers; to hit the ground with a sickening thump! With a hint of victory glinting in its eye, the stag prepares to charge for the final kill.

Kesh had lost his spear during the battle, but this fall has brought him within reach of it. Aching all over, he painfully rolls and grabs hold of the spear with the agility and speed of a professional warrior. Lifting the point now and bracing the spear butt on the ground barely in time, for the stag is almost on top of him. The beast runs straight into the spear, puncturing its brave heart.

The beast makes one final deafening bellow, as blood pumps out onto our hero's sweating face. And with one last sickening shudder, the beast falls to the ground dead.

> *In the middle of the journey of our life*
> *I came to myself in a dark wood*
> *Where the straight way was lost*
>
> Dante, the divine comedy

Kesh is triumphant. With adrenaline still pumping through his veins, he tears the antlers from the beast's head and places them on his own. Thus, by some mystery which we cannot tell, Kesh the Sun King becomes the Stag King, the representative on earth of the horned god - Cernunnos.

In the centre of the forest, he stands tall, powerful, and alive with the raw energy of life itself. Never has he felt so vital, so alive. He revels in this feeling for quite some time allowing the animal's stamina and energy to flow right through him; he is exulted.

Eventually, the light begins to fade. In the west, the sky became a purple bruise spreading wider until the sun gave the lighting of the world over to the silver wheel of the moon; which rose almost full in the east. His tribe always had special ceremonies when the silver goddess was full. They had named her Arianrhod. Her brooding light shone down on him now. Awakening strange animalistic feelings within him.

For the first time, since he donned the stag horns, he looks about him, and notices that he is, in fact standing in a small stone circle of squat grey stones within the poplar grove. In the silver light of the moon, the stones somehow remind him of human figures, small hooded monks in long grey robes. Then before his mystified eyes, the stone monks started to move. Slowly at first but circling him, they strike up a mournful chant as they slowly progress around and around him.

Gradually, the hooded monks pick up speed, going faster and faster. The chant, too, becomes faster, till it sounds more like the baying of dogs, for dogs is what they have become.

Beside him, the stricken stag, miraculously back to life, suddenly jumps up and with a quick, sure-footed bound, flees into the forest. The grey monk/hounds increase the pitch of their baying to a frenzied howl, then suddenly break off and pursue the fated stag into the silent forest.

The mournful baying of the hounds in chase gradually fades into the distance. Puzzled by all this, Kesh now finds himself alone once more in the Poplar Grove.

.

CHAPTER 16

Gorse

For several days, our young hero Kesh having now become Cernunnos, travels through the forest ever westward. Eventually, the land starts to rise steeply, the trees thin out and the way becomes rocky and more difficult.

The Sun is shining brightly, but less intense now as it loses its power during the autumn of the year. Up ahead Cernunnos could see a collection of gorse bushes. The bright yellow flowers look so full of life and abundant vitality that it draws his attention. The glowing flowers seem to be spots of yellow light like little suns, stirring and tossing about in the wind. It brings joy to his lonely heart just to behold them.

As he gets nearer the bush, several of the little yellow suns seem to break away. They fly about moving playfully, tumbling over one another, till they come near to one of the silver fir trees. Cernunnos watches fascinated by these little lights as they now dance about each other, comically leap-frogging one another.

Quite suddenly, they all stop as if played out. Then they start falling silently like little yellow snowflakes onto the grass at the base of the ancient fir tree. Disappointed that the show is over, Cernunnos moves a little closer straining his eyes to see where they may have gone to. As he nears the ancient tree, he notices what seems to be a pair of eyes in the trunk which as he stares, blinks at him. A little startled, he stood back but then noticed that the eyes were part of something not unlike a human head. Little by little a small human-like creature is revealed which seems to be part of the tree. She lays drooped over the inclined trunk, the wood nymph almost peels herself off the tree. He can now see her features more clearly, she seems to be a youthful girl, but her naked body is so covered in mud and clay and bits of moss, that he could hardly see her skin. Her red hair is wiry and full of leaves and twigs. She has little pointed ears that poke out from her haystack hair. There is also a hint of a small pair of horns like those of a young deer. Her slanted, green eyes, green as grass, are full of mischief and blink like those of a cat as they look at Cernunnos.

Behind her, another Fay creature appears from the tree. She stares at him like a timid animal. Then another head emerges from the trunk and more random hands and feet appear, till half a dozen Fay creatures are standing before him.

Suddenly they all start talking at once, laughing and giggling and pointing little fingers, like excited school children who have spotted their favourite pop star close by. They all come running over, chattering all the while with high-pitched giggles, stroking his skin, and his branching horns, which are now firmly rooted to his head.

Quite suddenly, as if by some unseen signal, the wood nymphs all become silent and still, standing before him. Then one of them, who has long curly bronze-coloured hair right down her back says, "Greetings Lord, wither ye go on this day of days"

Cernunnos, feeling now like a detached observer, heard his voice say in the same formal tones, "Hail creatures of the fir tree, I thank ye for your kind welcome. My time is done in this world, now I need to hide my face in another realm. For the Winter Queen has business here. I must continue my quest in the underworld."

Spirit Quest: The Heros Journey

He paused for a moment and then continued. "Loyal creatures, would ye lead me to death's doorway?"

The same creature as before answered, "Aye Lord, 'tis our duty and our honour."

With this, the formalities seemed to be over, for they reverted to their giggling and chattering, but all the while coaxing and leading him along a small pathway.

Shortly they came to a great mound covered in prickly green Gorse bushes. The bright yellow flowers were so abundant and bright, that it looked as if the very Sun had buried itself in the earth, with but a small segment showing above.

He was ushered to one end, where a collection of large boulders were visible. It was here they stopped. Then quite formally each of the Fay creatures came to him in turn and kissed him on the lips saying, "Fair thee well Lord."

When each had kissed him, they all held hands making a circle about him, then chanting in unison:

"Corn and grain, corn and grain,
All who fall shall rise again.
Hoof and horn, hoof and horn,
All who fall shall be re-born."

Over and over, they chanted, spinning wildly around and around. It was so exhilarating, such energy and power were generated by their joyful chanting and dancing, that Cernunnos thought that they could go on forever.

But gradually the singing and dancing stopped, and when they had regained their breath, they all chanted a familiar farewell, "Merry meet, merry part, and merry meet again."

With this, they all joyfully clapped their hands together and ran off into the forest.

Now once again he was left alone. He stared at the place where they had vanished for a few minutes, then smiled at the memory of them, shaking his

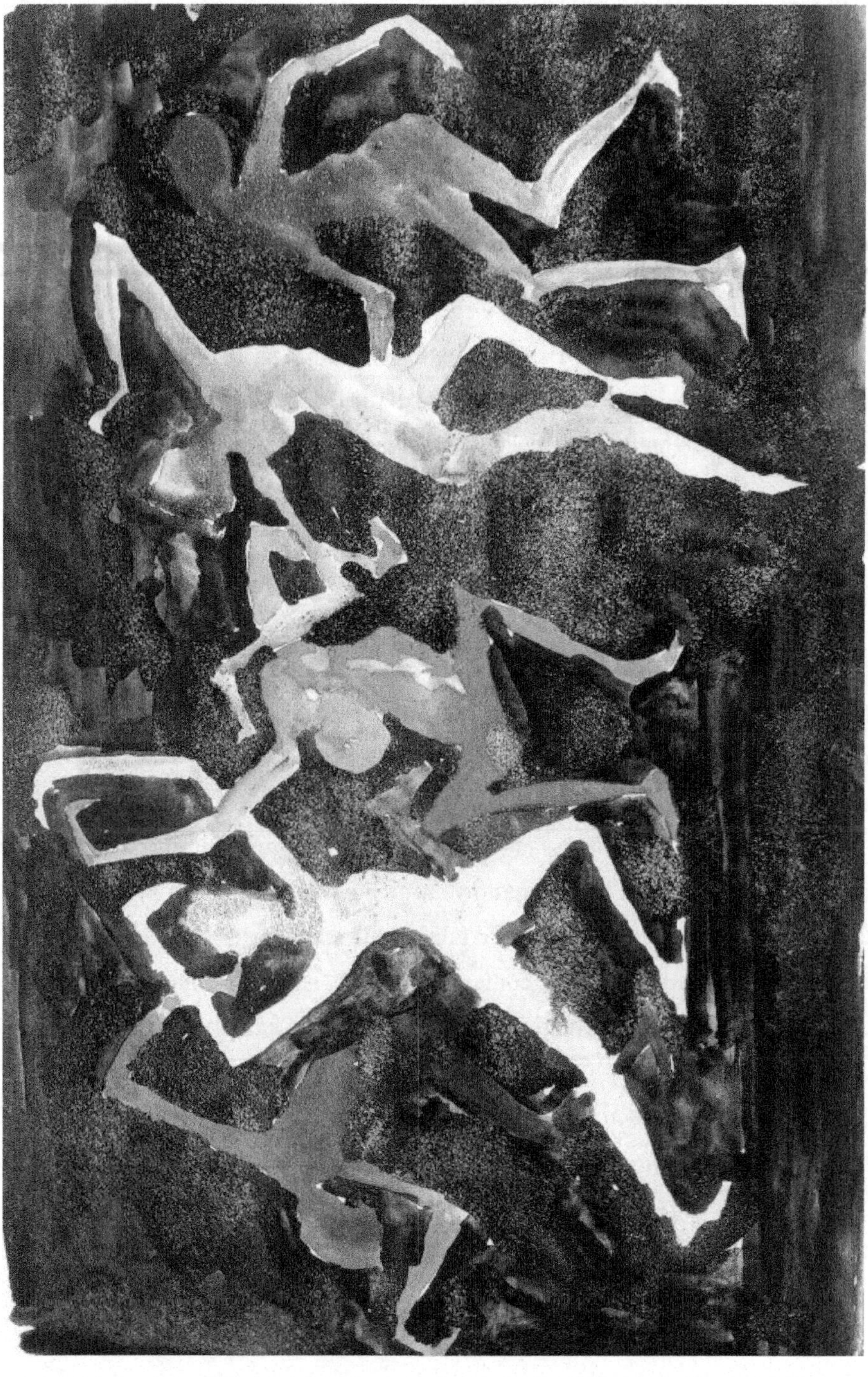

head, he turned to face the Great Barrow.

Amongst the boulders, a huge stone had been moved to one side, revealing a dark cave-like entrance, its dark depths stood open ready to enter. Above the entrance roughly carved in the rock is an image of an old woman squatting, as if giving birth, she is holding open her vulva. Cernunnos remembers he had seen one before, knowing it as Sheila-Na-Gig, the mother goddess giving birth to the cosmos.

Cautiously he walks over to the entrance, standing before it; knowing he must enter. After a small ritual that the old shaman had taught him, he asked permission from the barrow guardian, if he could enter this sacred place. Sensing no feeling of rejection, he slowly and reverently enters.

Inside, the walls are smooth and white. The rock is encrusted with millions of large and small crystals of quartz, glistening in the reflected sunlight. Looking closer he could see that the rocks contained many fossils of the spiralling ammonite type. These could be seen covering the roof above and on both side walls. As he walked further into the darkness, he could just make out carvings and paintings of intricate spirals and zigzag patterns. He knew that the spirals represented the spiralling earth's energy, and the zigzags represented underground water.

Continuing along the passageway he enters a larger vaulted room. In the centre of the floor is a large, shallow stone bowl, containing a pool of clear green water. Small drops of water fall into it from the crystal roof, with a noise like soft music. Light comes in from a sloping shaft in the roof, causing reflections from the pool and crystal ceiling, making a very pleasing effect.

Off to one side, is another smaller, darker chamber and when he looks into it closely, he can see a dark shape within it.

"Welcome," a small pretty voice comes from the darkness. "I am the spirit of the barrow. You are Kesh who has become Cernunnos."

"How do you know who I am?" he answers wonderingly.

The spirit of the barrow laughed with delight, "Why, Lord everybody knows who you are. All the forest animals and nature spirits are talking

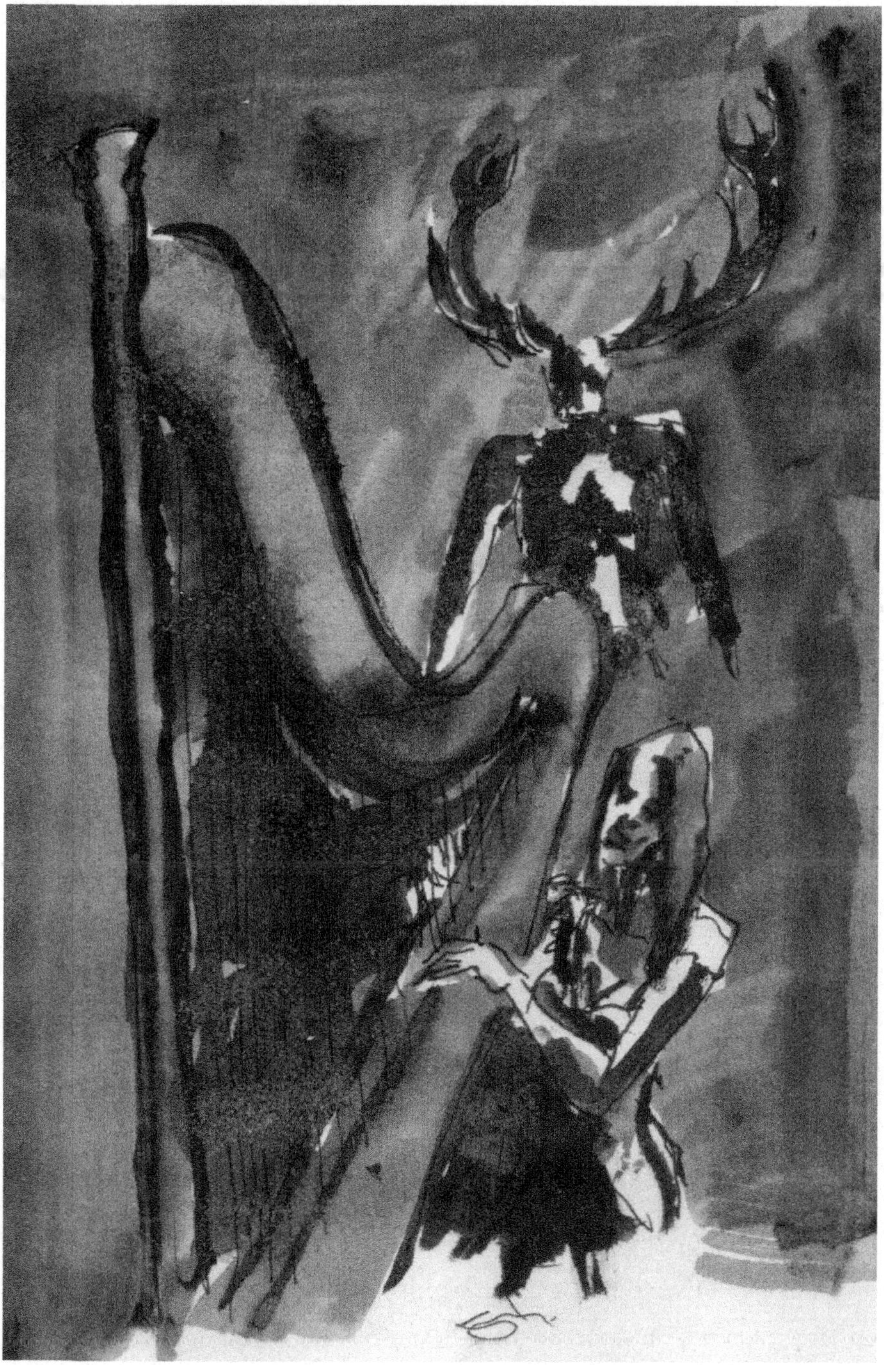

about your great journey. We have all been greatly impressed with your integrity and bravery, for is it not for us, that you partake of this Vision Quest?"

"This is strange, for I thought I was all alone in this thing," answers Cernunnos.

"Nonsense. We, none of us are alone on this planet full of fruitfulness and life. You have been granted great honour, you are the 'chosen one'. It has been your destiny from even before your birth, that you should leave the earthly plane and venture forth in search of your true consort.

"Be glad 'tis you. Be glad that in so doing, we can welcome in the destroyer, knowing that the seed is in the ground and that you will have the honour to fertilize the womb of the Mother. Come springtime, new life will be reborn from the fruit of your loins and the womb of the Earth. Now it is time".

After a few moments of silence, the sound of an elegantly played harp drifted through the stony barrow. It was the sort of harp that the travelling Bards had played in times long ago. She played good music. The music induced great gladness, but also great sorrow. She played the harp like he had never heard before.

Cernunnos closed his eyes and relaxed. Then laying on the floor he made himself more comfortable.

... Cernunnos travelled with the music, feeling so relaxed... the harp music took him to places and situations in his life. Places that seemed ordinary and plain to him, with no significance on their own...

The delightful harp music continued to wash over him. It was so relaxing, he felt himself melting into the floor.

... But within these ordinary situations, when seen in context to all the others, there seemed to grow new meaning and purpose to each one...

The hypnotic harp music continued to wash over him. He was so tired now, melting into the floor. So tired, but he felt so relaxed.

... There appeared to be a pattern in his life and now he could see it. Now he knew that it all had purpose and meaning...

Melting, sleeping - blissfully tired.

... And that everything that had happened to him had happened to bring him to this level of understanding; to this very point in his life...

Drifting, floating, flowing. Down and down he went.

Then he gradually realised the harp music had stopped. He felt a cold draught on his skin. Slowly he opened his eyes... a strange landscape met his gaze.

CHAPTER 17

Pine

The air was intensely cold. The stars, severe and bright. High above, the last rags of scurrying clouds raced past the moon in all her wildness. Not the voluptuous moon of a thousand southern love songs, but the Huntress, the untameable virgin, the spearhead of madness... it looked like an Omen... wildness crept into his blood. Cernunnos, found himself lying on his back looking up at a sky that was swept almost clean.

The spirit of the barrow had used her magical harp to transport him to the underworld. How this happened, he did not know, but he had ceased to be surprised by such things. So many surreal things had happened to him on his journey so far.

The young God stood up and surveyed the landscape before him. It was a strange, unfamiliar landscape. Gone were the familiar home-land forests of Oak and Ash. This was a cold land. A land of lakes and evergreens; high moorlands of purple heather, gorse, and broom. Beyond this lay jagged purple mountains capped with snow; they were all around him.

He stood on a small flat plain among the mountains. Nearby, he notices an arc of grey boulders and realizes he is standing in the centre of a sacred stone circle. In the moonlight, they look like grey-hooded monks, crouching to protect themselves from the coming night.

A strange Deja vu feeling comes over him and he thinks, 'Surely, I have seen this place before, but I can't quite remember where... But wait, what's that noise; it surely was music.' As it came again, he recognised the high-pitched reedy music of the pipes drifting softly through the chill air; by this time, it had almost become a friend.

But now, now he could hear another sound. Baying. Yes, the baying of hounds in the chase. It was so distant and so faint that it could only be heard when the wind blew his way; it was a mournful sound. He strained to listen, but now it was gone. Cernunnos shivered at the memory, that had nothing to do with the chill wind that blew down from the mountains in the north.

The young God with the branching stag's horns raises his nose to sniff the air; nostrils dilating like an animal. 'The frost Giants will join me tonight,' he thinks to himself. 'And winter will not be far behind. The Winter Queen will soon be passing over this land. Wherever I am, I need to find shelter tonight and warm clothing too.'

So, leaving the stone circle behind, he heads for lower land. Yet strangely, although he has an awareness of the cold; for he is still naked. He does not seem to feel the cold. Looking down at his naked body, he notices that he seems to have grown a thick pelt of chestnut hair. 'Stranger and stranger,' he thinks, as he continues his descent into the wooded valley of conifers.

Just as he starts to enter the woods, an almighty creaking, like that of a falling tree, issues from somewhere nearby. With lightening reactions, he stops in his tracks, turning towards the direction of the noise; ready to jump away.

But no falling tree does he see but an ancient Cedar with a distinct knotty face on its side. It is all covered with moss and dripping with ferns, the face had a very jovial expression.

"Welcome sir, 'tis a while since we saw the Lord of the forest come this way, but I must say 'tis a pleasure; yes a very great pleasure." Said the tree with the creakiest voice Cernunnos had ever heard.

"Ah! Touchwood. What a pleasure it is to see your gnarled old face," he found himself saying. "I have come in search of my Queen; the great wheel has turned yet again."

"'Tis so, my Lord. But wait, I have a friend of yours who will keep you company on your way".

The tree-being made the most appalling creaking sound as its branches moved this way and that as it muttered to himself, "Where is that confounded bird."

"Caw! Caw!"

Startled, Cernunnos looked up toward the sound, high in the tree.

"Caw...Caw..."

"Looks-far? You old crow, how did you get here... is it you?"

"'Tis me all right, but I'm not sure about you, with those antlers stuck on your head... Caw... Caw."

Cernunnos instinctively puts his hand to the horns on his head; he has almost forgotten about them. Then laughing, "It is good to see you, Looks-Far old friend. Here in this strange land, it's good to have someone familiar, to travel with."

"Caw... Caw! Your Lady awaits your coming... She needs a worthy consort... She has been searching this land, all over for you."

"Then we had better be on our way," And without another word, Cernunnos strides off into the woods, turning to shout over his shoulder, "Goodbye Touchwood, Thanks for your help."

> *The love that moves the Sun*
> *and the other stars*
>
> Dante; the divine comedy

Cernunnos and Looks-Far travelled for many days in the strange land.

As Lord of the forest, he never seemed to tire or never was hungry. He met many strange creatures along the way and stopped to chat with some of them, but always his burning drive moved him on and ever on.

The Centaurs, he liked very much but would not wish to have them as an enemy. The Fawns were kindly and warm. He also met a stallion unicorn once, who travelled with him for a while, and even let him ride his back for some of the way. But it kept looking behind and became skittish and timid, saying something about, "They are too close now."

The unicorn eventually ran off into the woods with a hasty goodbye; Cernunnos saw no more of him. More and more, Cernunnos found that he had just been going along with his instincts. He discovered that there were many things that he just seemed to 'know,' without ever having been told. Or rather, his body just seemed to know. It knew exactly what to do and which path to take; if only he allowed it a slack rein.

But with this growing 'instinct,' had also grown an uneasiness, a growing sense of foreboding. He couldn't name it but began to understand what the unicorn had meant; 'something,' was close and it made him jittery.

One cloudy, moonless night, when the wind was blowing from the south, he heard the very faint baying sound again, coming and going with the wind, it was from a very long way off.

It had been a full moon, the day he arrived in the stone circle. The silver Goddess had been high in the sky, shining like a great lantern, lighting his way during his night-time walking; for since the start, he had needed no sleep.

But, as is the moon's nature, she had been steadily waning; and last night she was almost spent. So, he knew that tonight she would be dark. His growing sense of foreboding had something to do with this night; he couldn't explain it. So, he followed his gut instincts. Tonight, he would not walk but strike camp.

He had stopped in a small clearing and gathered wood for the fire. Instinctively, he had gathered seven different herbs and seven different kinds of wood: Juniper, Yew, Pine, and Ivy - seven in all. He roasted a wild

Hare over the fire.

Earlier that day, he had spotted the Hare, which just seemed to have given itself up to Cernunnos. One minute leaping along. Next, it lay down in his path. When he got to it, the animal was stone dead. Cernunnos was grateful for the offering, so he slung it over his shoulder; it had been delicious roasted over the coals.

Now his belly was full and he lay by the dying fire. He tossed the seven gathered herbs onto the glowing coals. With a hiss, the pungent incense of the seven herbs washed over him like a perfumed wind. The fragrant incense was shrill in his nostrils, sharp, wild, and strange.

He had not slept for a fortnight, but now he was grateful for sleep. That night in the dark of the moon, he dreamt:

... Through swirling clouds of mist, high upon a ridge-way stood a solitary tree. He recognized it as a Scots pine. It could be seen for miles about; it was a marker tree. In the dream, his consciousness was floating high above; it drifted closer to the tree. He could see there was a figure tied to it, a man hanging there... The mist swirled obscuring his vision, but he was certain he had seen something on the man's head... a crown of thorns... or was it a crown of horns? Somehow, he couldn't remember... But then the clouds cleared again, briefly, and he could see the face; it was himself. It was himself hung upon that solitary tree.

There was such pain on that face, he could feel that pain now in his bones and a terrific thirst; such thirst. He knew he had been there for days; he was weak, almost at the point of death. Strange animalistic memories came to him now...

He could sense all the life in the forest... the powerful forces of nature awakening after winter slumber... irrevocably flowing like green serpents coiling and spiralling through the earth... A herd of deer comes crashing through the undergrowth running along paths that are older than the forest itself... all about him deer moving on silent slender feet... Now he ran with the deer, driven by the awakening earth energies of birthing spring...Running with the deer, swift and strong...the deer following the antlers of the horned one... racing with them speeding down the hillside. He was aware, as the herd was aware of the endless chain of life-- live, feed, bear offspring and die; and be eaten in turn to feed the children of the mother goddess.

But then he heard the barking cries of the hounds in the chase behind him. Ever closer they came... he could hear shouting voices, "Hark, there is the Horned one. This is the god the consort of the maiden goddess."

Then the darkness of the forest closed over him and swallowed him...

He was out of his body now, his consciousness floating above, looking down at himself hung upon that solitary tree. But below at the base of the tree; there were figures gathered there.

One was a young maiden in long robes of pure white. She had the most beautiful face, like a girl in a pre-Raphaelite painting. She was sitting on a stone, a bride stone. A horse-like beast lay beside her, a unicorn, its head in her lap and she soothed it and stroked it behind the ears.

Another figure there was. She stood in a long flowing dress of red silk. Her breasts and belly were swollen; the fruits of love were growing in her womb. She seemed to be glowing, radiant in her beauty; a ripe fruit blooming, almost ready for harvest.

A third woman stood there. She was a very old crone of a woman, dressed in a long black cowl. She stooped and leant on a knurled old stick, and she had a raven on her shoulder. Her hands and face were so old and wrinkled, they were almost as black as the raven. Yet something about the face gave him to think that she was a sister to the other two.

The vision was fading now. He could feel his life force ebbing, 'his' life, draining away. And with it, the vision was fading. Till all he could see was a diffuse white light all about him like a cloud; but there was a brighter light ahead. A blinding white light. He was coming nearer to it; he wasn't ready to go to that light. He tried to move away from that light. Summoning the last shreds of his will, he moved away from the bright triangle of light.

Now he could hear the echoing voice of the shaman taunting, "Answer me a riddle; what takes five steps to the left, then five to the right, then five

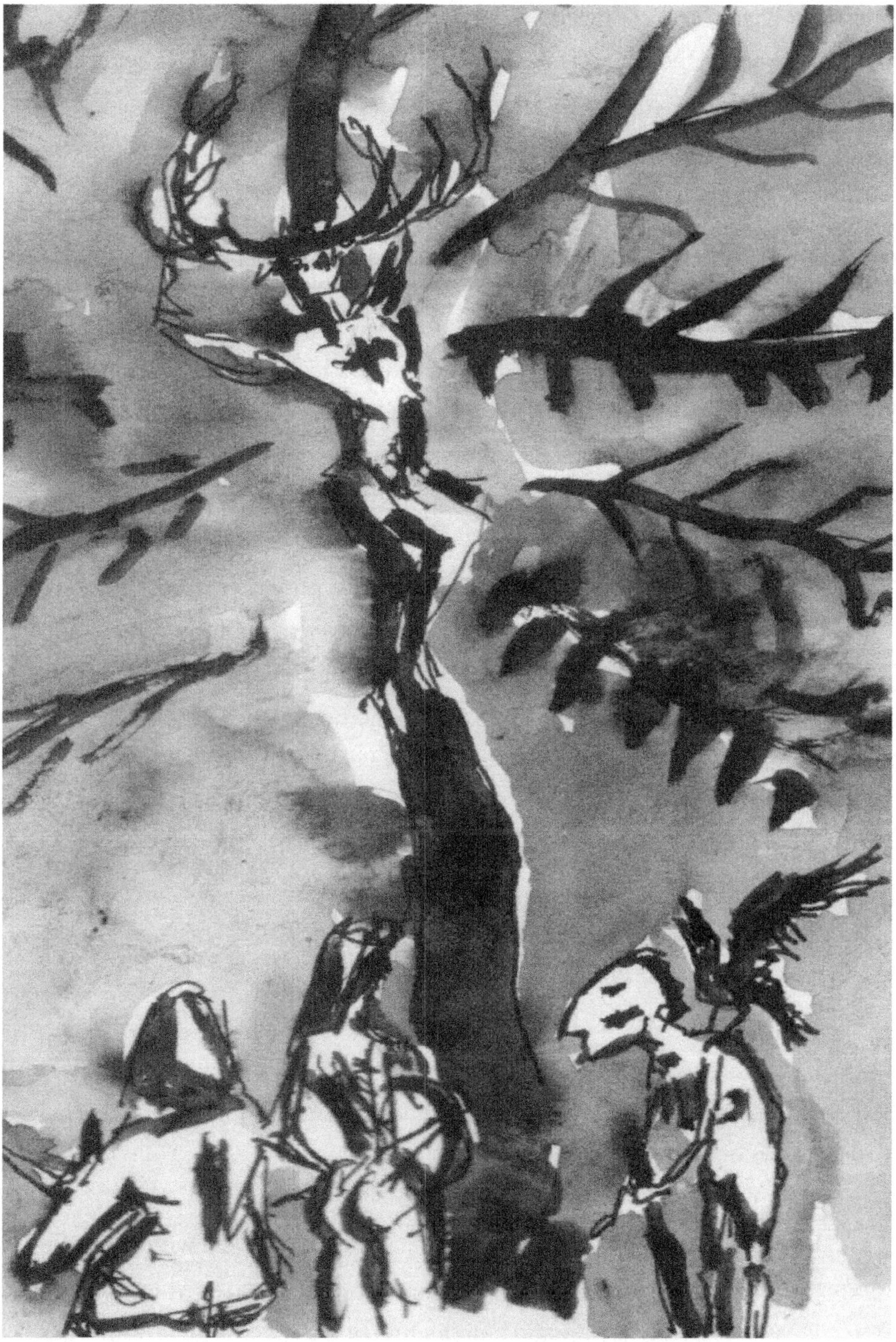

straight ahead, and another five at a skew? Don't know?

"Answer another then. Question: what has many keys but cannot open a door? An Ash tree you say. Not so. Ash has many keys; each will unlock the mystery of the Ogham. The salmon's sage wisdom is crystallized within the trees of the Ogham. Yet each tree contains a twentieth part thereof. 'Tis where we Druids of old gained our fabled wisdom. 'Tis still there today. For the bold warrior to gain. With the Ogham as your key, you can unlock the wisdom contained in the trees. All you need do is go ask..."

The next thing he was aware of was a gentle hand soothing his brow; it felt good and healing. Beneath him, he could feel soft furs. He felt warm. A bowl was placed to his lips, he could taste cool clean water and so allowed a few drops to pass his parched and cracked lips; he was too weak to do otherwise.

Slowly, he opened his eyes. He was in a snug little cave, hazily he could see the smiling face of a maiden greeting him. It was the face of the young woman in white robes, in his dream. Skin so white, eyes of hazel, like deep pools of compassion and hair like wild honey, freely flowing down her face and shoulders.

"Who are you... I mean...? I saw you in my dream," he managed to say.

"Hush brave warrior; my name is Olwen and 'twas no dream."
She looked at the puzzlement on his face. "Yes, that was you hung on that tree. An initiation many don't survive. You, yourself were so close to death's doorway... but we got you down in time."

"We... but how? Who...?" he blubbered.

"T'was the hounds who put you there, the hounds of ignorance. Even though you went underground to the underworld; they followed you. They caught you in the end."

"But... why?"

"Because of who you are, the Stag King. You are the King who wears the crown of horns - the antlers of seven tines. In a way, you put yourself there too, in your search for truth and enlightenment. In a world of darkness and ignorance, you shone so brightly that you blinded some of them; they felt they had to douse your light. When you move in their world, you need to shield your light. Shine out too brightly and they may crucify you. But enough talking now you must get your rest."

But Cernunnos was already asleep, exhausted by his ordeal. The young maiden lay her head down beside him, content.

CHAPTER 18

Elder

On a rocky limestone hill stood an ancient elder tree. So old was it that it seemed part of the rocky outcrop; its thick trunk ribbed and gnarled with age. A tangled mass of roots flows along the rock's face seeking tiny crevices, forcing their way deep into the earth.

Children gather here in the springtime when the tree becomes a mass of small white blooms. They are picked by eager children, just for the fun of eating flowers. Or maybe as a special treat, dipped in a thin batter and shallow fried; with a squeeze of lemon, it becomes a picnic feast.

Adults, too, pick the flowers, which are quickly fermented into fragrant, fizzy lemonade which delights and tickles the noses of innocent giggling girls.

Young lovers gather under the shelter of her branches, in the early evening, drawn perhaps by the erotic smell of her blossoms at night. Here, they may quaff cupfuls of the light but heady wine that has a sensuous smell and sweet taste of flowers; brewed by the more patient, from those same white blossoms. The eager, amorous, young men plying liberal cupfuls to their lusty, young maidens; and delighted, watch their corks POP!

Later in the autumn, that same Elder tree produced a multitude of jet-black berries. These could be gathered by the more experienced, for these, too could be fermented with honey to produce red-gold mead. Which when aged, fully, resembled port and would be appreciated by the more mature pallet.

Below that rugged tree, hidden among the folds of rock and foliage, there was a cave. A secret place, seemingly shallow, but a small hole high at the back leads down, deep into the earth. The narrow passage follows faults in the ancient limestone created by aeons of flowing water, scouring deeper and deeper. Sometimes horizontal, then suddenly falling vertically for fathomless depths, only to level out again.

Occasionally water pours out from a side passage. An underground stream follows our path till it tumbles headlong down a hole in the floor. All about are formations like ice flows. Stalagmites and stalactites and columns of lime, created over thousands of years by dripping water seeping through from the surface. We follow the passage further down, deep into the womb of the Earth.

Eventually, we come to a cosy circular chamber lit by a small lamp. In one corner there is a bed with many furs; on it lays a man sleeping. On his head is a set of antlers...

When next he awoke, Cernunnos was alone in the snug little cave. Slowly and painfully, he sat up and looked about him. It was quite dimly lit, but there was an oil lamp burning in the corner. By its light, he could see that he was in a cave, and he knew somehow, that he was deep in the earth, for it was so silent.

He was so stiff and tired that he could not move from the bed of furs, so he just lay propped up on his arm staring at the lamp. Although his body was tired, his mind was strangely lucid. Thoughts of what Olwen had said to him passed through his mind.

As he watched the lamp, a moth drawn to the light, circled the small flickering flame. Making large circles at first, then drawing nearer, flying faster and faster working itself into a frenzy; till it almost touched the flames.

'What,' Cernunnos thought, 'Drew it to the flame? Perhaps it was an awareness of the light. Or perhaps it is the heat that draws them. That small lamp in the darkness of the cave must seem like a thousand suns, to a Moth.'

He thought again about what Olwen had said of his search for enlightenment, and a wry smile came to his lips. 'We know very little of man really,' he thought. 'Many men, he knew, would go seeking the truth, but we don't know if they could actually see it. Perhaps man cannot see truth. Perhaps nature has denied us that gift. Perhaps, we can sense only its presence. Perhaps, we can sense only its heat. Perhaps, to stand occasionally in its presence is sufficient. Perhaps, if a man touched it, they would die burning in its flames.'

"Why so pensive Lord," said a woman's voice nearby.

Cernunnos almost leapt off the bed, so deep in thought was he, so unexpectedly had the voice spoken.

A dark-hooded figure stood before him; he had not seen anyone enter; maybe she had been there all the time. He was sure it was a woman's voice, a very old voice; but still full of power. The figure wore a long dark cloak, with a hood pulled over her face so that it could not be seen.

"Who are you?" He asked, surprised.

"Welcome to my domain, Lord. I am glad you have recovered from your ordeal. As for who I am, do you not know me, Lord? For it is I that you have searched for, all through your great adventure." She cackled a laugh, seeming to find some comic irony in her comment.

"I have many names, in many lands, but you may call me Ceridwen."

Cernunnos paled, for he knew well that name and feared it. She cackled again, with some private amusement. Then, out of her cape came a bony finger and gestured that he follow. Incredulously, Cernunnos watched the old woman take a branch from the floor, which instantly burst into flames. Then she walked into a dark passage, which he had not noticed before.

With great foreboding, Cernunnos silently follows. He follows her down a steep incline. Eventually, the narrow passageway opens into a small grotto lit by torches. Beside the entrance, carved into the naked rock is a figure he recognizes. An old hag, with a triangular head and bulging eyes, she squats down, revealing her vulva, which she opens with her own hands. Water flows from her yawning Yoni into a cauldron carved below. To one side is a crescent moon that looks like a boat with a star above it. On the other side is a sickle. The symbolism isn't lost on him, for the old Druid had trained him well.

As he peered into the dimly lit grotto, he could see that the floor of the cave was strewn with bones. In the centre, is a fire and placed on the fire is the largest cauldron Cernunnos had ever seen. It is made of burnished bronze and has intricate designs etched into its sides. Interweaving knots and animals, crescent moons, and sickles; around its rim are inlaid pearls.

The hooded figure stands by her cauldron of transformation. Then she pulls back her hood, revealing the wrinkled face of an ancient crone.

"Come, Lord, into my inner temple, we have much to learn."

In awe, Cernunnos cautiously joins her by the cauldron and peers into its depths. Some liquid is steaming and bubbling in it but seems to glow with a light of its own. The hag waves a withered hand across its surface; which instantly stills.

The surface of the brew becomes like a mirror, and he can see his face in it. It was much changed from the one he knew before he set out on his quest. Far older and wiser it was, but there was still a youthful look to his skin and features. A beard, too, had grown, and his eyes were so clear and soulful and wise. On his head, he could see for the first time the twin antlers.

Yes, he had changed; he was not the same person who had set out on this journey. Somehow, seeing it on the outside, helped him realize how much he had changed on the inside, too. The transformation was awesome. However, he became aware that Ceridwen had come to stand beside him. She put a comforting arm around his waist, but he was too wrapped up in his thoughts, to notice that she too was looking into the cauldron.

"Do you recognize him?" asked the crone with great compassion in her voice.

"Hardly, I have changed so much."

"Yes, the boy became a man. And now the man has become a God. No longer are you Oisin the boy. Lord of the forest are you; a true and worthy consort for the Goddess. All seem to know it but thee," she spoke with amused irony.

Cernunnos sensed what the implications of this talk meant. And suddenly realising her intimate closeness, became a little uncomfortable. For the implications were that he was to be the consort to the Goddess - Ceridwen.

This meant that they would be hand-fasted and become husband and wife. And that they would need to... 'mate' together... But she. She was so very, very old. He had thought that the goddess would be... well... beautiful... and to be blunt, young. How could he... God or no God... he just couldn't.

Ceridwen, all this while had been watching him closely. Understanding his conflicting emotions and thoughts. A wry smile came to her face.

The young God looked again at his reflection in the cauldron. The deep dark eyes, the tanned skin, the thick curls of his beard. Despite the changes, he was still young and... she... she was so very old. In panicked desperation, he turned to look, for the first time at the crone's reflection in the cauldron. But instead, what he saw was the face of Olwen - the beautiful young maid he had seen when he first awoke in the cave. He had fallen hopelessly in love with her, from the moment he first laid eyes on her. Seeing her again, his heart skipped a beat. Blood started pounding loudly in his ears. With joy in his heart, he looked up quickly, preparing to embrace her; but all that he found was the old crone.

Confused, he looked down at her reflection again and sure enough it was Olwen there on the mirrored surface. Three times he looked up and down again; thoroughly confused he was. The young face of Olwen broke into a beautiful smile and rippling, joyous laughter filled the cave.

Then she spoke with the voice of a laughing young woman, "I am sorry Lord to have put you through this; but after all this is the Cauldron of transformation and change."

She composed herself, suddenly more serious. "You are of the Sun, my Lord; you have seen steady change as the year progresses. But I? I and my sisters are of the moon; we are constantly changing. We three are separate but all-of-a-one.

"Lord, to gain your heart's desire, to gain enlightenment and become consort to the trinity of the Goddess. To partake of the Great Rite, the Sacred Marriage, you need to embrace this mystery; you need to embrace all three sisters.

"But experience has shown us, that what men find most difficult, is to embrace the Crone. This is your final task."

When she had finished speaking, she moved slightly away from the cauldron and looked at him. He too looked up, and for the first time looked earnestly at her old face. She put a bony hand to her throat and untied a cord there, causing the cloak to fall to her feet. The old crone stood there naked before him in the firelight.

He looked critically upon her, without emotion. He could see the fine bone structure, the high cheekbones. Yes, she had been beautiful once, indeed exactly like her younger sisters.

He looked at the bony, withered, old body; that by some mystery had given birth to the other two sisters. The sagging, empty paps; that had fed and nurtured her children. The loose skin hanging from her old bones. Despite all this, she still had the bearing of a Queen.

Overcome by a sudden moment of madness, he fell to his knees. Then lay down prostrate on the ground in front of her, embracing
her feet and kissing them, saying, "Blessed be the Holy ground you walk upon."

Then kissed both her knees, saying, "Blessed be thy knees that kneel before your cauldron altar."

Kneeling before her, he kissed her sacred Yoni, saying, "Blessed be thy

Spirit Quest: The Heros Journey

womb that had created all life on Earth."

Kissing her breasts, he said, "Blessed be thy breasts that have fed and nurtured the children of the Earth."

Finally, saying, "Blessed be thy lips that have spoken the holy words and breathed life into your creation." With this, he put his strong arms around her, embracing her body. Closing his eyes, he kissed her on the lips. He could feel her respond to him, moving to place her arms around him. He felt her shift in his arms, and when he opened his eyes again, he saw, to his great surprise, that he was holding the young maid Olwen.

Through bewilderment, came joy. Through joy, came strength. He took her up in his strong arms and carried her to the sleeping furs beside the fire, laying her gently down.

Olwen looked up at him and smiled, took hold of his hand, and pulled him to her, "My Lord, congratulations, you have won your Queen and I too have found my worthy consort."

Then she kissed him fully on the lips. They embraced and kissed again and again, coming together in ecstatic joy and bliss for many a long hour.

Always that faint surprise. Distance slightly dazed
is your sweet shock stalked deer caught in light beam
lightly vacant gaze. So known yet so still amazed
at my pride, unfurled and raised, which you do esteem
and fain to praise, star-wondered with your open stare,
your urging eyes so virgin wide could hold the sea
and all the sky, yet praise me just by being there.
Adored at how your awed at what's about to be
is such reward; to see you thus, so trembled, flushed.
So cupid arrow quarry quivered, so frisson fraught,
so bull-rush tamed, so chaste and gamely maiden blushed.
So lost and found! - Oh, how delicious you are caught!

High above their heads, on a green stony hill stood a solitary Elder tree.

A cold wind howled down from the North, blowing through its barren branches. In the village nearby the Halloween 'bone fire' was burning. Children danced about it, singing happily the Rhymes of old.

Some older children came through to the fire, carrying a man of straw; throwing him onto the flames to cries of, "The king is dead - long live the king."

CHAPTER 19

Blackthorn

A savage, bone-chilling wind had been blowing all night long. But now all was still, as the gloomy first light of a winter's dawn, revealed that the first snows of winter had fallen on the purple mountains to the north.

The silver ball of the sun hides behind thick layers of grey clouds, that swirl and scud across its sunny face. Its melancholy light produces little by way of warmth and comfort. As it somehow seems reluctant to rise too far above the horizon, staying low in the sky all day.

Before us, the reeds and bulrushes of a marshy fenland, stand still as death above the boggy waters. Scrubby bushes of blackthorn, protect their purple-bloomed, bitter fruits with savage thorns.

All animal life seems to have withdrawn to a safe hiding place. Only those nature spirits and dryads that have learnt to withdraw their vital life forces, deep inside their roots will survive this winter. Those who leave themselves exposed will wither and die. On the foothills, the leafless trees stand stark against the winter sky, like skeletons, quiet and still, all seeming to wait.

Suddenly, in deathly silence, a confusion of mist secretly steels down from the snow-mantled mountains. Slowly rolling and folding over boulders and trees; full of wispy shapes and Sylphs. All that the frigid mist touches becomes white and frost-fettered.

Gigantic, dark shapes seem to move within the mists. Spectral shapes of Elemental frost giants, secretly doing their work under its concealing hand. Their chieftain, Jack Frost, touches his icy fingers across trees and bush. Spreading layers of hoar frost everywhere he goes, though he is an 'underling,' prelude to the Winter Queen.

Suddenly, a hyperboreal blast blows down from the mountains. Frenzied clouds that have been swirling around and around the highest peaks, break away and come tumbling headlong down to the valley below. Freezing snow driven by the wind, streaks down at acute angles, which quickly piles up in drifts against everything that lays still.

Deep in the snow-laden clouds, there is a dark, stormy disturbance of energy, boiling red and black, spewing forks of lightning in all directions. A black form can be seen moving within, and at times we receive fleeting glimpses of an ancient crone, riding a gigantic snow-white goose.

As she rides across the land, the snow goose ruffles her plumage, creating clouds of feathers which fall as snow. The crone is the Cailleach; she is Chaos. She carries a long black staff, her Blackthorn rod of power. The rod is 'The Destroyer.' It can destroy established order. As the Cailleach rides, she cracks her black rod against the frosty ground, trees, and lakes. Lightning bolts of power emanate from that rod. With her coming, all turns to snow and ice, destroying all life as she goes.

Beneath the snow-covered thatch of the Great Hall, the old Shaman sits staring into the central fire; warming his old bones. He is wearing thick furs and sitting close to the fire, yet still, he can find no warmth. He listens to the icy blasts howling above the insulating thatch and wonders if he will make it through yet another winter.

The cunning man knows there is deep strife and testing times ahead.

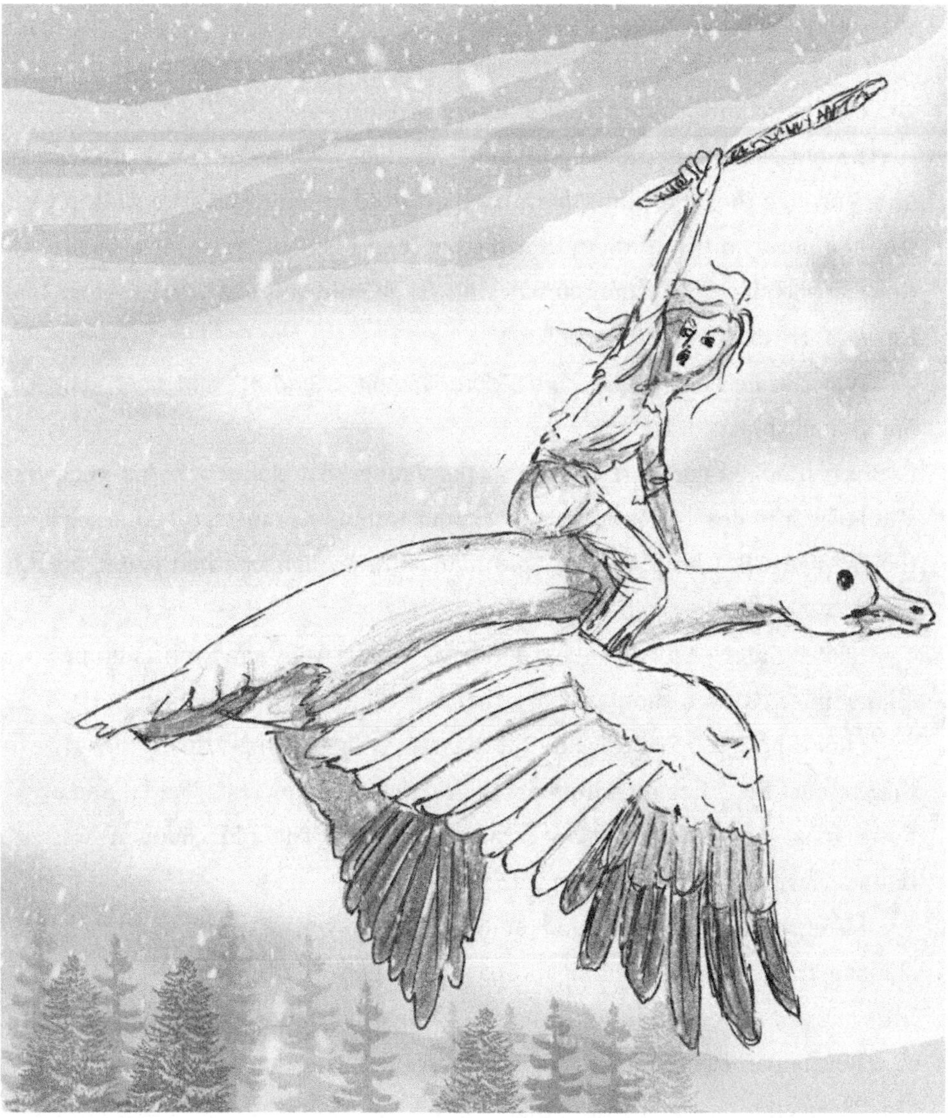

For there is a very real danger in the deepest winter, that the weakest of the tribe may die. The very young, the old, the sick - may perish.

"Emrys, tell us another story. Emrys," shouts Moss, a young six-year-old boy.

"Oh yes, yes, another story. Oh, please Emrys," calls Hazel, a pretty little girl, clad in fox fur, which matches her russet hair.

The old Shaman, smiles indulgently at the children gathered around him. Through the long winter months, they loved his stories before bedtime, seeming never to tire of them. But the old man casts an eye over to young Rowan, who sits alone, silent and downcast. "Would you like another story, Rowan?" He calls over to the boy.

"Why did he have to die - old Robin was my friend, it's not fair?" The boy sullenly blurts out.

Emrys looked compassionately at the young boy. Robin was his uncle and loved him dearly. "Yes, I'm sorry about Robins passing too," confessed the shaman. "But he was a very old man, Rowan, his time had come. He couldn't take another cold winter."

"I hate winter! Why do we have to have winter? Why can't it be summer all the time?" Rowan shouts sulkily, then bursts into sobs of anguish.

"I know how you feel Rowan. But that's the way of things, this is the way things must be. After the summer, the earth needs her rest... and... and... there must be dark to balance out the light." The old Shaman was floundering, his old brain numb with the cold.

"Listen, come gather round and I will tell you another story," the shaman tries a more familiar approach. "Perhaps you may understand a little more at the end of it, for it is a story about the creation of the world..."

The shaman cleared his throat and settled into the storyteller's cadence. "In the beginning. In a world that was not our world, for it was a place without time or substance; there lived a Dragon. She was black as coal, yet everywhere she went, there was snow and ice. It was like this from the very beginning of time, for countless Aeons.

"However, by some mystery, it came to pass that the black Dragon gave birth to two other Dragons. A red Dragon and a white Dragon. The little Dragons were very happy and played with each other for centuries; for these creatures are very long-lived.

"But eventually they grew up, and as is the nature of beasts, they mated. Now a strange thing happened, for wherever they mated, the physical world came into being; around the place where they joined. And this is how our world started. And the more they mated, the more the physical world grew and grew.

"The black Dragon, being ancient and wise, knew that there could never be limitless growth in any world. So, at regular periods, she came into the physical world, to destroy some of what the red and white Dragons had created.

"She also decreed, that the red Dragon should live in the Earth and rule the time of growth. And that the white Dragon, should live in the sky and rule over the time of abundance. And so it has been ever since. So you see my friends, the need for all these aspects in our beautiful world. But as we are also part of this world, we must abide by those rules. For as it is in the world about us, so it must be within each of us."

As the shaman finished, he closed his eyes, seeming to sleep. Each of the children where silent now; they were well used to these sorts of stories from the Old Druid. It helped prepare them for the realities of life and the reasons things went as they did sometimes.

Whether they truly understood all they heard, is a guess I cannot make. But you can be sure that each child went to bed that night, dreaming of Dragons.

In another world, deep beneath the earth in a cave, a man with branching horns and a beauteous maiden could be seen making bountiful love, on thick layers of fur. The seed of the God planted firmly into the fertile womb of the Earth Goddess.

Root and stone and water and earth;
The seed in the furrow,
The beast in the hole.
The leaf on the tree gives itself to the ground,
All to rest and forget,
Deep under the snow.

CHAPTER 20

Reed

It was the deepest winter, just before the longest night. The land lay locked in snow and ice. It had so far, been a long, hard winter and all the signs bode there was more to come.

But for the moment, there was a lull in the snowstorms. Three brave huntsmen had taken their chances to go hunting for fresh game to feed their hungry tribe. These hunters were good men and well-respected by their fellow tribes' men.

Oak was strong, good-looking, and sturdy like his name. Ailim was tall and slender, and some said he had a faraway look in his eyes. Gort was an artisan; he loved working with wood, and it was he who had made the longbows which all three men carried.

These bows were made of the finest yew wood. Strung with gut, and each hunter had a quiver full of reed arrows, straight and true, with flint tips and goose quill flights. Each man was proud of his skill at arms, but prouder still of their expertise in the long bow. With a clear line of sight, it was quick-flying death to any quarry.

When hunting larger game, they would tip their arrows with a swift-acting poison distilled from Yew berries. This would ensure the quarry was brought down quickly and not be lost to the forest. Yet, each knew that such game needed to be roasted and not boiled to destroy the poison.

On this particular occasion, the hunters had been lucky and gained a good-sized hare and a couple of wild turkeys. But they were looking for larger game, for it would soon be Yule tide and the midwinter feast. The hungry tribe needed a good feast and celebration at this bleak time of year. But before they feasted, they would not sleep during the longest night, they would be praying till dawn; calling for the return of the life-giving sun. If the gods willed it and the newborn sun did return from the underworld, there would be great celebrations and feasting and exchanging of gifts.

Beforehand, twelve days before. The tree's roundabout would be hung with mimics of fruit or other food representing the abundance of nature that they wished to bring back. Shining balls, too, would be hung and candles or lamps in honour of the sun.

To the tribe, the sun was all-important. From its warmth and light; all life came. The whole tribe prayed and meditated, willing to bring back the sun; they wanted to bring back the sun. For in those days, winter could be a desperate time; many went hungry. The weakest died.

The tribal memory was long, too, and it remembered back to a time, long ago when the sun did not return; the time of the Great Ice. Sometimes, if the winter was particularly hard, they would go out and fetch an evergreen sapling and place it in the village centre. In the old days, they would use a young Yew tree; a reminder symbol of the continuous cycle of life - death - rebirth.

This tree would be honoured and decorated with bright things and golden orbs. Winter greenery would also be brought into their homes: holly, ivy, and mistletoe. For within these trees were thought to be the life forces of the god and goddess. Therefore, they would be welcomed into their homes and honoured and kept warm and safe away from the death and destruction of the Winter Queen.

When the snows had receded, the spirits could return to the land in the

127

bright fires of Imbolc. The regenerative and creative force of the Goddess in the ivy; the star seed semen of the God in the mistletoe; the spirit of their newborn sun in the holly.

At this solstice celebration, a great 'bone fire' of oak would be burnt, in the centre of the village. All the individual hearth fires in each household would be extinguished. The old ashes would be cleared away and later scattered on the fields. The base of the hearth was a big oaken timber buried in the ground. It would smoulder away all year long. But at Yule tide, it would be dug up and a new oak base laid in its place. These old Yule Logs would be brought out and taken to the central fire and burnt with the rest of the villager's Yule Logs; bringing unity to the whole village. 'Out with the old in with the new'.

During the festivities and dancing, the oldest son of each household took some glowing coals from the main fire. These would be taken to each hearth fire in turn, for it to be re-lit. And so the new year and the new sun were welcomed in. So began a new cycle...

The three hunters were still tracking for deer; they had been out for several days now and were cold and weary.

It came from the north. Oak heard it first. Initially, he thought it was some kind of bird song, in the silence of the snow. But no, the melody dipped and shifted, sometimes low, and breathy now high and skirling. He looked about him and could see that his companions had heard it, too. Ailim and Gort silently stood, facing north, listening. As the pipes wandered up and down, the music scale, always low and quiet, just on the edge of hearing.

For Oak, it brought a deep yearning with it. A primal thrust of passion came over him; he could feel his loins stirring and his manhood hardening. Suddenly he had an overriding desire to be with his wife, Elfie; to hold her and be passionate with her like never before.

Gort reacted differently to the music. He had an impulse that he should be home finishing a wooden sculpture he had started. He felt an overwhelming need to get a knife in hand and to whittle slivers of wood away. To reveal the rounded shapes inherent in the wood; just waiting there to be discovered.

Ailim was unable to describe his feelings. He only knew that as the music played, it was like somebody had suddenly turned on a light inside him. He could feel it radiating from his very being; it seemed to light up the winter gloom about him. If you looked upon his face, on this cold winter day, you would see his skin glowing radiant and a light in his eyes, as he looked in Awe at something above him.

We follow his gaze to the cliff face above.

There, stood, magnificently regal and silent was a giant stag. His imposing antlers, a full seven tines. This sudden close encounter with a large, living, breathing creature was overwhelming for the hunters. The vibrant life force just seemed to exude from the beast.

With the snow and ice, and winter destruction all around him. When all other animals were tucked away in burrow, hole, or nest; somehow, he survived in the open air. Surely there was God force within him. Certainly, he was King of the forest. There he stood, high above them, a majestic King; with a crown of horns.

All three hunters stood transfixed. Awed and fascinated by this Holy sight. Not one reached for an arrow or bow. Then suddenly it was gone. Stag and music had snapped away like it had never been.

Like waking from a dream, the men looked about them dazed. As snow began gently falling in soft flakes to the ground. All three turned as one and walked back to the village in silence.

Deep in the centre of a circular earth mound, was a corbelled chamber. In that chamber sat a dozen holy men and women, waiting. Waiting for the return of the Sun. The chamber had been constructed long before anyone could remember. Some say it was made by Faeric folk. Others by a race of sorcerers and magicians before the coming of the Celts.

The mound was covered with white rocks. So, from a distance, with the sun shining on it, it resembled a giant white egg, half buried in the earth. A long, thin passageway linking the central chamber with the outside had been aligned to the winter solstice sunrise. On that day's dawn, a long shaft of sunlight would penetrate into the womb of the earth and illuminate the chamber with glowing golden Sunlight.

But now the Druids waited and contemplated during the long, longest night; in the dark. The air was thick with aromatic herbs and the smoke of exotic fungi. As they sat there in the darkness, they contemplated; they contemplated the past; they contemplated the future.

The longest night, in the deepest winter, is a time, out of time. On the Celtic medicine wheel, this place is the place of the silent warrior. The place of deep contemplation and reflection. It is a place of looking at yourself in the mirror and assessing yourself openly and honestly. Have we achieved what we set out to do last year? Have we directed our life from spirit? Have we allowed our instincts to guide us? Have we allowed our ego to have free rein and allowed it to take us where it would? Or, have we used that charging team of horses, kept them in check, and under control, but allowed that energy to take us to where we want to go?

Where have the reed arrows we aimed so carefully landed? Or did they go astray, lost in the bush? Did you get lost in your own labyrinth, that you wove so tightly about you? Did you get distracted by life's various delicious fruits along the way; forgetting your Quest entirely?

And what of the future?

Now, in the silence and stillness of deep winter, we can craft our plans for the future, coming from this place of spirit. Having gone through the trials and tribulations of a complete year and not being 'in' the actual 'doing stage.' We can see more clearly the greater whole and direct our lives from spirit.

Deep in the earth mound during his contemplation, one of the Shaman druids received a vision, quite unlike any vision he had received before:

... He saw through the misty vision, a man with a set of deer antlers on his head. He was tied to a tree; he looked to be dead... Now he was in a cave, vibrant with life again, for the god was making love with a beautiful young goddess... Time moved on again. Now, the goddess was with child... she was giving birth, on a soft bed of furs... Now the god with antlers held up a newborn baby boy, whose brow shone like the sun... The scene changed again, and the God and the Goddess were placing the child in a small round boat, setting him afloat on the water of an underground stream... Now the psychic vision of the Druid moved to outside the cave, where three hunters approached the stream, at a narrow ford... The same baby had floated downstream and now lay in its tiny craft caught in the Bulrushes. A small bird was perched on the rim of the coracle, looking inquisitively inside; the bird was a Wren. It flew off as the baby cried out... now one of the hunters was kneeling before the baby's craft...

But the Druid's vision was fading now; he saw no more, "What did it all mean?" He wonders.

No fire or light was allowed into the Holy chamber of the barrow, but water in great stone bowls was heated by hot glowing, egg-shaped stones that were heated in a fire outside. The cooled eggs were replaced repeatedly by druid apprentices. The whole effort causes an effect like a sauna or sweat lodge.

When the first light of the winter solstice's dawn, caused golden shafts of sunlight to enter the passageway, it penetrated through this hallucinogenic haze of smoke and steam. The golden shafts Illuminate the chamber, refracting through crystals hung from the roof and reflecting from the water basins, creating a veritable Mardi Gras of light and colour.

With the dawning of the sun after the longest night, the Druid Shaman inside were sure the sun had returned at last. Great whoops and shouts could be heard from inside the barrow.

This signalled to the people gathered outside to sound the great bronze horns that would fill the dawn. In turn, alerting all that the new sun has been reborn... Rejoice and celebrate. The sun has graced our land again...

Happy suns return... Many happy returns of this day.

Then the dancing could begin. The singing and merry-making, too. The banging of drums and a great cacophony of noise set up; which would carry all across the country...

"Everyone rejoice, let the feasting begin ... "

THE END

Appendix

Notes on the Celtic Medicine Wheel

The natural world works in circles and spirals. The spinning of the Earth brings the cycles of day and night. Earth's orbit around the sun brings us the seasons. The moon's cyclic motion around the earth creates her changing moods and phases of the moon.

Not surprising then that many ancient traditions have created a circular medicine wheel based on the natural world and land where they were living. They do this in a bid to integrate themselves and better understand the changing moods of the natural world where they live.

The Celtic medicine wheel then is a symbolic representation of the elements, seasons, directions, trees, animals, and wisdom of the lands in Ireland, Scotland, Britain, and parts of Europe. It is a tool for self-enquiry, guidance, and healing that connects us with the natural and spiritual forces of nature

I will explore the main features and meanings of the Celtic medicine wheel, and how it can be used for personal growth and transformation in another of my books.

As explained in the preface this particular book focuses on the sacred trees of the Celtic Medicine Wheel. And how we can utilise their medicine to work with male rites of passage. The hero sets off on a vision quest in the form of the sacrificial king.

However, in a bid to better understand some of the symbolism entwined within the story, I feel it important to explain some of the aspects of the Celtic medicine wheel here.

Misinformation

But first, it is as well to be aware that there is a lot of misinformation and misguided arguments on-line (and in books) regarding the Ogham and the so-called 'Celtic tree alphabet. Most of the misinformation can be traced to Robert Graves's book 'The White Goddess' first Published in 1948.

To quote from Wikipedia: "Robert Graves was a poet and novelist who proposed a theory of the Celtic tree calendar... However, his theory has been widely criticized by scholars and experts for being based on faulty sources. Graves' version of the tree calendar is not a reliable or authentic representation of the Celtic culture, spirituality, or cosmology. It is more a product of his own poetic imagination and personal agenda."

Unfortunately, Graves' work on the Celtic tree calendar has become a mainstay of new-age spirituality and has consequently been used as the basis for many proposals for the Celtic medicine wheel.

Qualifications

I have personally worked with the Ogham and the trees associated with it for over 50 years. I have cut, carved and worked magically with every tree associated with the Ogham. I have crafted numerous Ogham Fews and lots with the correct woods, all 20 of them. This involved countless hours walking the woods and forests of this Celtic land, identifying all 20 trees with leaf, bark and branch. As well as all that I have taken my Ogham divination sets to countless psychics and mystics fairs (and other festivals) divining for countless people. All the while learning more and more about the wonderful symmetry woven into the Celtic medicine wheel that I use.

Consequently, I feel qualified to comment on the validity, formation and use of the Celtic medicine wheel. I hasten to add that this is not my proposal. I have utilised the work laid down by several serious researchers who have attempted to uncover the secrets of the medicine wheel. However I have, through continuous use in divination, meditations and other magical work validated that this system 'feels just right' and seems to work on many different levels. So many in fact that I feel it is beyond the human mind to create such a system, and therefore truly believe it has been retrieved from the Otherworld.

Directional Correspondences

In its most basic form, the Celtic medicine wheel is divided into four quadrants, each corresponding to a cardinal direction, an element, a season, a time of day, a stage of life, and a quality of being. For your convenience, I have also included the stations of the Ogham trees around the wheel see the enclosed figure.

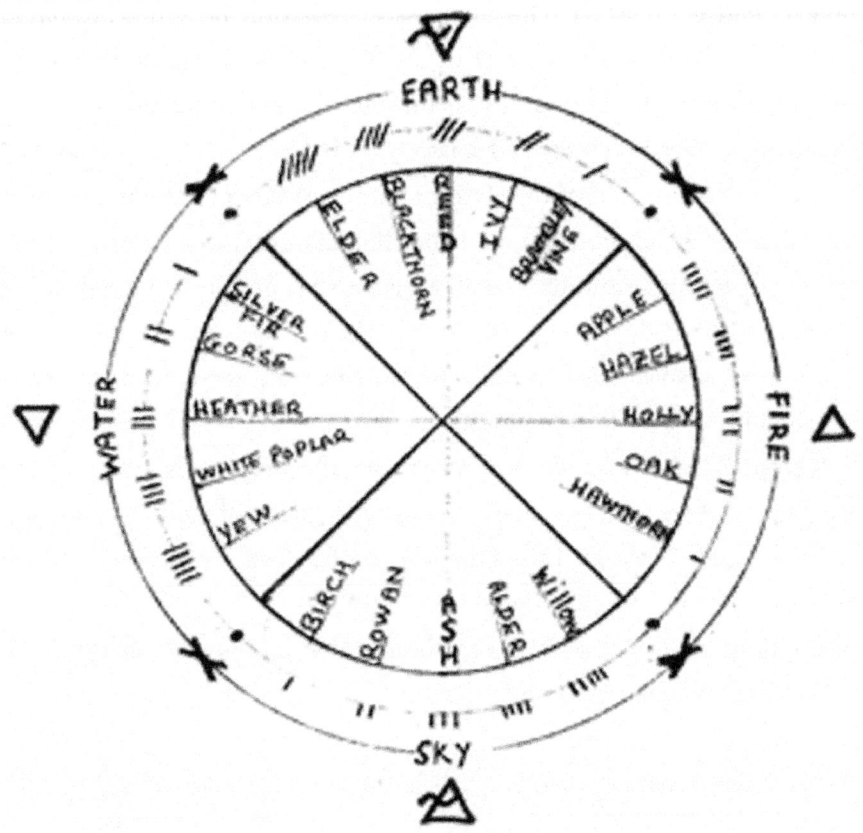

The four directions are:

East: The direction of the rising sun, the season of spring, the time of dawn, the stage of spring of your life - childhood to teens. Quality of intellect, mind and inspiration (fire in the head). This is the place of new beginnings, fresh ideas, and creativity. The trees associated with the east are apple, hazel, holly, oak and hawthorn. Element of fire.

Note: Notice here the wonderful symmetry of opposites within the wheel;

fire opposite water; and earth opposite sky.

South: The direction of the midday sun, the season of summer, the time of noon,

the stage of summer of your life - youth and manhood. Quality of willpower and passion. This is the place of Doing and action. Energy, courage, and enthusiasm. The trees associated with the south are birch, rowan, ash, alder and willow. The element of Air, however, the more encompassing quality here is 'Sky' as this includes not only atmospheric air but emanations from the sky and stars.

West: The direction of the setting sun, the season of autumn, the time of dusk, the stage of the autumn of your life; maturity. Quality of emotion, feeling, empathy, intuition, healing, creativity and a balanced inner harmony.

The trees associated with the west are silver fir, gorse, heather, white poplar and yew. The element of water,

North: The direction of the midnight sun, the season of winter, the time of night, the stage of tribal elder and old age. Quality of stillness, patience, endurance and reflection. This is the place of the silent warrior reflecting on the past, and contemplating the future.

The trees associated with the north are elder, blackthorn, reed, ivy and bramble. The element of earth.

The Celtic medicine wheel also has a centre, which represents the spirit, the source, the void, and the oneness of all things. The centre is the place of balance, harmony, integration, and transcendence. The world tree is associated with the centre, the axis mundi, and the bridge between the worlds. In Celtic mythology, this is often associated with the Ash tree.

The animal associated with the centre is the serpent, which symbolizes the life force, the cycle of creation and destruction, and the spiral of evolution.

As mentioned above the Celtic medicine wheel can be used for various purposes: meditation, ritual, journeying, healing, and learning. If we align ourselves with the energies and teachings of each direction, we can gain insight, guidance, and empowerment for our personal journeys. As the story of our hero sun king shows us it also connects us with the trees, animals, ancestors and spirits of our land. So we can learn from their wisdom and medicine. In all, the Celtic medicine wheel touched on here is a living and dynamic system that invites us to explore, experience, and express our true nature and potential. It is a sacred circle that honours the diversity and unity of life, and the interconnection of all things.

Notes on the Ogham

The ancient Ogham alphabet is considered by scholars to be the earliest known form of Irish writing. Often called the 'Beth-luis-nuin' alphabet or the 'Celtic tree alphabet'. Old Irish and Ogham being the Secret Language of the Poets.

The alphabet glyphs are represented by a varying number of strokes and notches marked along a central drum line (see figure). The system lends itself perfectly to being carved on wood, bone or stones.

Most often though it is seen along the edge of megalithic stone monuments. These inscriptions belong to the 5th and 6th Centuries AD. Of the 369 known inscriptions by far the highest number occur in the south-west of Ireland. To the mind of modern archaeologists, nothing survives of the Ogham beyond these stone inscriptions. To those blinked scientists,

Birch
Rowan
Ash
Alder
Willow
Hawthorn
Oak
Holly
Hazel
Apple
Bramble
Ivy
Reed
Blackthorn
Elder
Fir
Gorse
Heather
Poplar
Yew

this is all there is to the Ogham, who then cast it aside as an outdated form of ancient writing.

However according to the Auraicept na n-Éces (an Old Irish text), Ogham was first invented along with the Irish language, by the legendary Scythian king, Fenius Farsa. The Scythians were a group of Iranian nomads, who inhabited the Eurasian steppes from about the 9th century BC.

Very few examples of Ogham carved on wood or bone have survived, as these materials are not preserved well. One of the oldest carved pieces of wood found in Britain dates back to more than 6000 years ago and has Ogham markings on it. There are also authentic references to the ogham mentioned in many of the old Celtic myth and legend stories written in the Book of Leinster and the Book of Ballymote. However here the Ogham is referred to not as writing but is used as magical inscriptions or talismans. From these legends, the invention of the Ogham is attributed to Ogma 'Sunface' who was a member of the Tuatha de Danann, a race that inhabited Ireland before the coming of the Celts. All this brings one to conclude that the Ogham is very old indeed and certainly from the pre-Christian era.

To mystics and modern druids, however, the Ogham is an ancient magical script used by the ancient Druids of Ireland. Modern druids believe that hidden within the Ogham is much of the lost Druidic lore. Ogham is believed to hold ancient cypher keys, which can enable, those with an open mind, to unravel much of the mysterious knowledge the ancient druids possessed. Much work has been done in recent years to unlock and decipher these ancient codes.

Most of this work is being conducted on a psychic and intuitive level and often uses shamanic journey work to retrieve lost knowledge. Consequently, we have discovered that the whole Ogham system is quite complex, and the learning of it by the ancient Druids was a primary aim, for it was used as a teaching model or mnemonic, for learning other facts as well as being a spiritual guide. The symbolism encompassed within each of the twenty Ogham characters is unique to each of the native trees and crystallises the essence and vibration of that particular tree.

Notes on The Stag king

The Myths and Lore surrounding the Stag run across the world from Meandash, the mythic Saami reindeer, all the way back to the earliest history from Sumerian.

From the Saami tribes, whose lives are reliant upon deer we can understand how central their knowledge was. When you, your family and your tribe's clothing, diet, tools and thus survival are reliant on a single animal then they become symbolic of life itself. By conjecture, we can imagine the same would be true of the hunter-gatherer tribes as they followed the deer north after the receding ice sheets of the last ice age. Thus Britain and Ireland would have been recolonised by these tribes and the folklore surrounding the Stag, Hart and Hind consequently have become an ingrained mythic symbol in Western society. Even today in such folk traditions as the Abbots Bromley Horn Dance, and even the bastardised form of the Santa Claus mythos.

Cernunnos, the Celtic Horned God was a Stag God and was depicted with the antlers of a stag; and seen to be a god of fertility and plenty, and the Lord of all animals, many people today link him with the Green Man.

And since their tribe lived by hunting and knew about the cycles of nature they also learnt the need for balance. They deeply respected the spirit of the deer herd in the form of 'the Stag God'. They knew the tribe must only take that which was needed to feed the tribe and no more. The tribe also abided by the natural law that: 'a sacrifice must be given for sacrifice'. Thus if the deer herd were to give of themselves in sacrifice for the tribe then to balance one of the tribe's very best hunters should be sacrificed to the spirit of the deer herd. So they devise a ritual whereby the one to be sacrificed, the very best hunter of the tribe should be treated like a king for the whole of the year and would be known as the Sacrificial King. And he, after his reign for one year should be dressed in deer skins and antlers placed on his head. And he was to run with the herd among the deer and be hunted by the tribal hunters so as he would know what it was like to be the stag among the herd. The hunter would become the hunted. And if during the hunt the sacrificial king should be trampled by the herd, he would be deemed the sacrifice demanded by the deer herd spirit.

But if during the hunt he was challenged by the king stag of the herd he should fight and if he won he would become the King Stag and the Stag God would flow through him and he would become a great leader of his people.

Notes on Vision Quest

Vision quest is an English-language umbrella term for a rite of passage in some Native American cultures. It is usually only undertaken by young males entering adulthood. Across the globe, many individual indigenous cultures have their names for their rites of passage. A few examples are the Australian Aboriginal 'Walkabout'- A journey of self-discovery and spiritual connection for boys, who must survive in the wilderness for up to six months.

Then there is the Plains Indians 'Sundance' - A sacred ceremony of sacrifice and renewal involving fasting, dancing and skin piercing. Then there is the more unusual 'Land-Diving' - A rite of passage for Vanuatu boys, who must jump from a wooden tower with vines tied to their ankles, their heads coming within inches of the ground.

Essentially such rites of passage like the 'vision quest' involve endurance like going alone into wild nature on a spiritual journey. The aim is not only to prove you can survive alone in nature but to seek guidance or insight from a spirit guide. During a vision quest, one may fast, pray, meditate, or perform rituals to connect with the spirit world to receive a vision or a message that can help one to discover life's purpose, identity, or direction in life. It can mark a significant transition in one's life, such as from childhood to adulthood.

About the Author

Corin Thistlewood has lived an eclectic life. He began his career as a successful aerospace engineer. However he had a deeply spiritual side as well, so followed his passion for Metaphysics & personal development. This eventually led him to qualify in several Alternative therapies including Shiatsu, Shamanic healing & Transpersonal hypnotherapy before opening the Australian College of Druidry, which was given the moniker 'the real-life Hogwarts by the media.

Corin now resides in South-west England, where he has become a full-time author. His literary works delve into captivating realms, blending elements of Shamanism, Celtic spirituality, and hypnotherapy.

www.corin-thistlewood.ueniweb.com

Blog: https://corin-thistlewood.ueniweb.com/blog#space

Facebook: Corin Thistlewood: Novelist | Facebook

About the Illustrators

Steph Minns has been a keen story writer and artist since childhood. Originally from the suburbs of London but now living in Stroud, UK, she spends her spare time writing, drawing and painting.

She worked as a graphic designer, illustrator and publications manager for many years in London, for charities such as The Prostate Cancer Charity and Stonham Supported Housing.

Her dark fiction stories range from urban and folk horror to paranormal crime thrillers. Steph's professional publishing history includes several short stories in various horror anthologies (Grinning Skull Press, Almond Press, Zombie Pirate Publishing, ParaABnormal magazine, among others). She has a novella published by Dark Alley Press (The Tale of Storm Raven) and a paranormal crime thriller novel (Death Wears A Top Hat) published by J. Ellington Ashton Press. Her two collections of short horror stories, The Obsidian Path and The Old Chalk Path, have attained 5 star reviews on Amazon. You can find more details on her website https://authorstephminns.weebly.com.

Jeremy Hughes artist, works largely as art director on community projects creating whimsical sculptures and illustrations. He is located in South West England and is available for commissions contact: albinogherkin@gmail.com

Printed in Great Britain
by Amazon